BHADREŚVAR

Bhadreśvar

THE OLDEST ISLAMIC MONUMENTS IN INDIA

MEHRDAD SHOKOOHY

With contributions by

MANIJEH BAYANI-WOLPERT

NATALIE H. SHOKOOHY

BRILL

MANOHAR

2025

Cover illustration: The Shrine of Ibrāhīm (Lal Shahbaz Dargah) and ruins of Solahkhambī Masjid, Bhadreśvar.

First published by Koninklijke Brill NV, Leiden, The Netherlands in
Studies in Islamic Art and Architecture: Supplements to Maqarnas series as vol. II in 1988.

This edition (2025) for South Asia is being published by
Manohar Publishers & Distributors by arrangement with
Koninklijke Brill NV, Leiden, The Netherlands.

ISBN 978-93-6080-448-0

Published by
Ajay Kumar Jain *for*
Manohar Publishers & Distributors
4753/23 Ansari Road, Daryaganj,
New Delhi 110 002

Printed and bound in India

CONTENTS

Part One

THE ISLAMIC MONUMENTS OF BHADREŚVAR

Part Two

A STUDY OF THE ISLAMIC INSCRIPTIONS IN BHADREŚVAR

PART ONE
THE ISLAMIC MONUMENTS OF BHADREŚVAR

MEHRDAD SHOKOOHY

THE ISLAMIC MONUMENTS OF BHADREŚVAR

INTRODUCTION

The site of the ancient city of Bhadravati, or as it has been known since the mediaeval period, Bhadreśvar, is located in the district of Kachh, on the north east of the Gulf of Kachh. The site is situated over one kilometre north of the present coast, 36 kilometres east of Mandvi and 20 kilometres north-east of Mundra.

Bhadreśvar has been known for its Jain and Islamic monuments since J. Burgess[1] published his first report on the site in 1875. Amongst the monuments Burgess mentioned were two old mosques, built with monolithic columns and roofed with flat slabs. He did not give any date for these structures, but his description suggests an early method. Furthermore, Burgess reported an old Islamic shrine, built with carved blocks of stone and bearing in his words "an Arabic inscription in square Kufic characters". The Kufic inscription was indeed another indication of the early origin of the building. Moreover it was an exceptional case in that no Islamic monument of comparable age was known on the west coast of India.

However, the greater part of the Burgess report was concerned with a local chronicle written in the early 19th century by the Jain Guru Bantvijaya and kept in the Vasai temple of Bhadreśvar. In the present report this chronicle will be referred to as the *Bantvijaya Chronicle*. It begins with the coronation of Raja Siddhasena at the port of Bhadravāti in the 12th year of the Mahavira era (c. 516 B.C.) and ends with the events resulting in the total destruction of the city and closure of its temples in V.E. 1907/A.D. 1850. This chronicle, recording the existence of a Muslim community at the site as early as the middle of the 7th century, speaks of a Muslim raid in V.E. 747/A.D. 690. However, the chronology of this account is regarded by Burgess as untenable. Elsewhere[2] he explains that while the writer of the chronicle has used every endeavour to trace the *ināms*, or royal gifts of land to the temple, he has tried to square his materials with the chronology. To accomplish this he has assigned reigns of 32 years and upward to all the earlier kings whose names he supplies, making 16 rulers cover a period of 900 years. Nonetheless the *Bantvijaya Chronicle* reflects genuine historical events, some of which are also confirmed by other sources, and will be discussed in the following pages. The presence of an early Islamic settlement is substantiated by such sources, and this question will be treated in some detail below.

In 1876 Burgess published another report[3] on the Bhadreśvar monuments where he gave similar accounts of the history except that the name of the writer of the local chronicle was given not as Bantvijaya but as (Jaina Guru) Khantvijaya. In this report Burgess studied the great Jain temple in detail giving drawings and photographs. For the Islamic monuments, however, he repeated the description from his first report without adding any new information.

For nearly a century no more attention was paid to the Islamic remains at Bhadreśvar, until 1965 when Dr. Z.A. Desai[4] published a study of the inscriptions. This study revealed that the inscription at the mausoleum, locally attributed to a person known as La'l Shahbāz, was dated as early as *dhi'l-ḥijja* 554/December 1159 to January 1160. Other tombstones found at the site also belonged to the same period, the latest being dated *sha'bān* 625/August 1228.

As is apparent from these dates some of the Bhadreśvar Islamic inscriptions are amongst the earliest in the subcontinent and as Desai has already claimed,

---

1 James Burgess, *Memorandum on the Remains at Gumli, Gop, and in Kachh, etc.*, Archaeological Survey of Western India (ASWI), Memoirs, III, 1875, 11-19.

2 J. Burgess, *Report on the Antiquities of Kaṭhiawād and Kachh*, 1874-5, ASWI, II, 1876, 206.

3 *Ibid.*, 205-10.

4 Z.A. Desai, Kūfī epitaphs from Bhadreśwar in Gujarat, *Epigraphia Indica, Arabic and Persian Supplement*, 1965, 1-8.

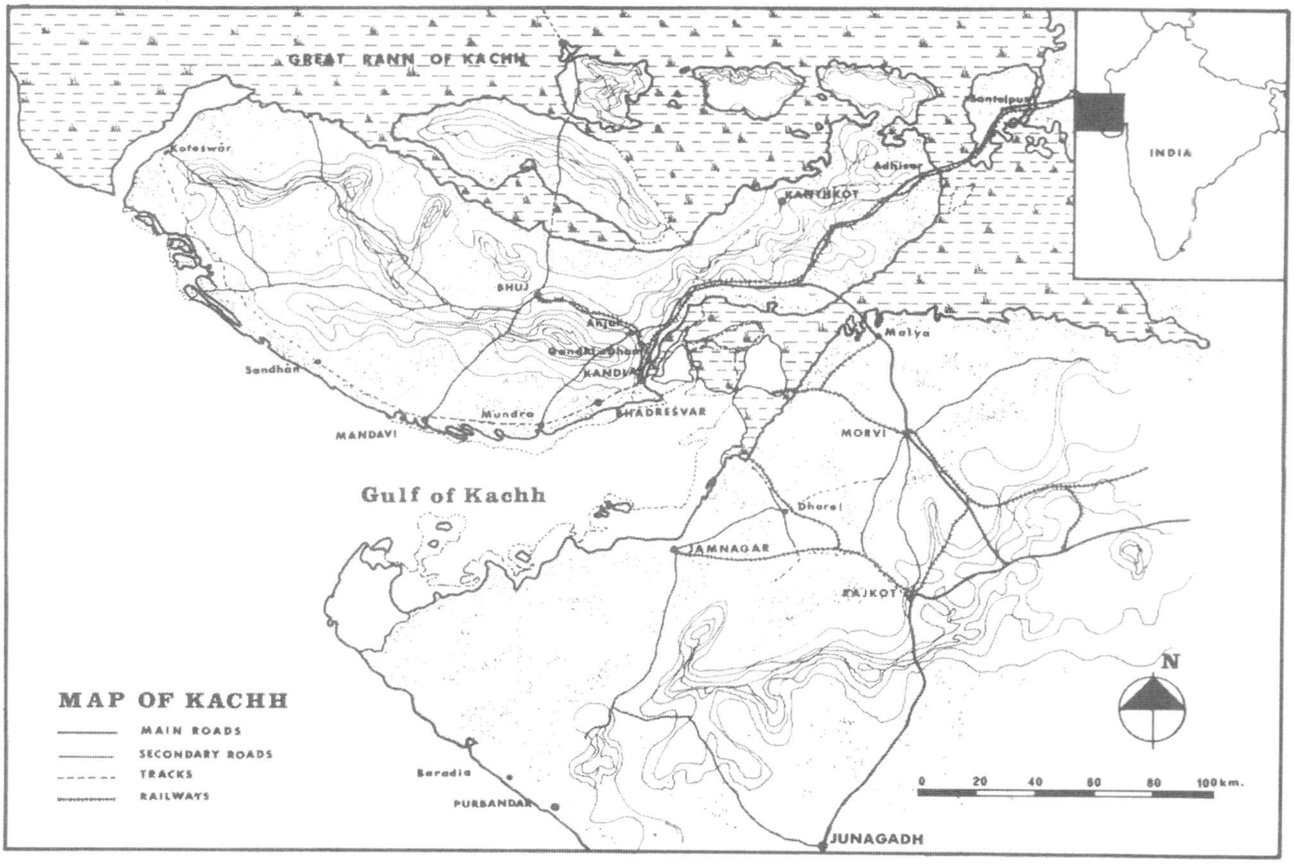

Fig. 1 Map of Kachh.

that of the La'l Shahbāz mausoleum is the earliest of its kind to have been found *in situ*. It is 35 years earlier than the Ghurid conquest of Delhi which was marked by the building of the Quwwat al-Islām mosque[5] in 592/1195, and nearly one and a half centuries before the conquest of Gujarat by the sultans of Delhi. The Quwwat al-Islām is usually regarded as the earliest Islamic building of India still standing. Moreover the history of Indian Islamic architecture is usually reckoned to begin with this building, which is considered to have inspired the style of all the later monuments.

However, the influence of the Islamic world in India obviously did not begin only with the Ghurid conquest. Since 93/711-12, when Muḥammad b. al-Qāsim[6] invaded Sind, an Islamic government remained constantly in control of that region. When Henry Cousens,[7] early in the 20th century, carried out the excavation at Brahmanābād (Bahmanābād) his work led to the uncovering of the site of al-Manṣūra, the Arab capital of Sind. During these operations part of an old building was found which Cousens regarded as having been the original mosque, built by the Arabs just after founding al-Manṣūra. The layout of this mosque was probably arranged on the traditional Arab plan which includes a central courtyard with surrounding colonnades, deeper on the *qibla* side. The

[5] J.A. Page, *An Historical Memoir on the Qutb, Delhi*, Memoirs of the Archaeological Survey of India, (MASI), XXII, 29. Maulvi Muhammad Ashraf Husain, *Record of all the Quranic and Non-historical Epigraphs of Delhi*, MASI, XLVII, 111.

[6] *The Chachnāma*, English translation by Mirza Kalichbeg Fredunbeg, Karachi, 1900, 93, 143 and 159.

[7] Henry Cousens, Brahmanābād-Manṣūra in Sind, *Archaeological Survey of India, Annual Reports* (*ASIAR*), 1903-4, 133-44; Excavation at Brahmanābād, *ASIAR*, 1908-9, 79-87; *The Antiquities of Sind*, ASI Imperial Series (ASI IS), XLVI, Calcutta, 1929, 50-1.

foundation excavated by Cousens was built of brick rather than stone, and nothing survived of its superstructure or decorations. The excavation did not include the uncovering of a *miḥrāb*, or the complete layout of the building. The true function of the building, therefore, remains to be determined after future excavations. The Jāmi' of al-Manṣūra is, however, recorded by the early Muslim geographers, amongst them al-Muqqadasī,[8] who gives an eye witness account of the building as it was in the middle of the 4th/10th century. He mentions that the mosque was built in the middle of the commercial centre of the town, and was constructed with stone and brick on a large scale with four entrances. Muqaddasī compares the mosque with the Jāmi' of 'Ummān.

An interesting point in Cousens's excavation was the discovery of three small mosques, which he did not describe in the report. He did, however, provide a photograph[9] showing the foundation of the *qibla* wall of one of the mosques which had a single *miḥrāb*, semi-circular in plan, projecting from the back of the wall. As we shall see, the plan of the *miḥrāb* resembles those found in Bhadreśvar, and may be an indication of the early date of the mosque uncovered in al-Manṣūra.

Between 1958 and 1965 during the excavations at Banbhore,[10] situated on the coast of Sind and most likely to be the site of the ancient town of Daybul, another early Arab mosque was found of which the earliest inscription dated back to 109/727-8. Unlike the Jāmi' of al-Manṣūra, the foundations are preserved in full. It was built on an Arab plan with rubble and mortar. Remains of some pre-Islamic reliefs on these stones, and a complete *linga* used as a step in front of the threshold are indications that the mosque was built with materials from Hindu temples. However, as at al-Manṣūra, nothing could be found of the columns or roof. Dr. F.A. Khan, who directed the excavations, suggests that they must have been of wood. An important feature of the mosque is the lack of any trace of a *miḥrāb* in the foundation of the *qibla* wall. Although the possibility of the former existence of one or more flat *miḥrābs* cannot be ruled out, Dr. Khan suggests that the mosque was probably earlier than the time when the tradition of building *miḥrābs* was established.

While the surviving foundations at Banbhore provide evidence of the type of plan in the early Arab mosques in Sind, the scanty remains of the superstructure both at Banbhore and al-Manṣūra are of little help in illustrating the Islamic architecture of the subcontinent before the establishment of the Delhi Sultanate. No other dated building of that period was known before the publication of Desai's report on the inscriptions of Bhadreśvar. However, his report was purely epigraphic and did not deal with the archaeological or architectural aspects of the monuments.

In 1977 the present writer had the good fortune to meet Dr. Desai, and to learn from him that some of the buildings were still in a good state of preservation, so that close study could be expected to throw new light on the origins of Indo-Muslim architecture. As a consequence, the writer was encouraged to visit Bhadreśvar in June 1977, and surveyed and photographed all the extant monuments. The present report is based on these researches.

Since the survey of Bhadreśvar the writer has been engaged in a project of surveying the sultanate monuments of north-western India, including the coastal area of Surashtra, Gujarat. In 1981, and during the field work in Junagadh, the mosque of Abulqāsim b. 'Alī al-Īrajī, closely comparable with the buildings in Bhadreśvar, was surveyed. The inscription of the Junagadh mosque dates from 685/1286-7, more than a century later than that of Bhadreśvar, but still prior to the take-over of Gujarat by the Sultanate of Delhi. This mosque is studied in an appendix to the present report.

HISTORY

The history of the city of Bhadravāti goes back to the period of ancient India. According to the *Bantvijaya Chronicle* the first kingdom of Bhadravāti was established on Thursday the 5th of *Chaitra Suddh*, in the 12th year of the Mahavira era (c. 516 B.C.), which is no doubt an artificially extrapolated date. Since this alleged period, the city remained a wealthy port and the capital of a state which at one time was said to have 97 towns in its territory. As explained before, the dates of this chronicle are unreliable; nonetheless it

[8] Shams al-dīn Abū 'Abdullāh Muḥammad b. Aḥmad al-Muqaddasī, *Aḥsan al-taqāsīm*, Leiden, 1906, 479.

[9] *ASIAR*, 1908-9, 136; H. Cousens, *The Antiquities of Sind*, pl. 8a.

[10] F.A. Khan, *Banbhore*, third revised edition, Karachi, 1969, 24-30.

reflects a belief in the ancient origin of the site: an opinion which is also confirmed by other sources.

One of the earliest sources to refer to the settlement is perhaps the *Mahābhārata*[11] which speaks of Bhadravāti in connection with the story of Yudhiṣṭhira's *aśvamedha*. According to this story the sacrificial horse for the ceremony had to be found in Bhadravāti. The *Mahābhārata* does not record the location of the city, but maintains that Bhadravāti is far from the Himalayas, and beyond Hastināpura, the capital of the Kuru kingdom, supposed to lie on the bank of the Ganges. The *Mahābhārata* Bhadravāti, therefore, seems to be comparable with our site in the district of Kachh.

It is interesting that Kachh is the only district in India well known in history to have a good breed of horses. This fact is recorded by several Islamic historians; amongst them Abu'l-faḍl[12] who writes:

«مغرب رویهٔ آن ولایتی است بزرگ جداگانه آنرا کچّه گویند ... بیشتر دشت و ریگستان. اسپ گزیده وتازی نژاد دانند و شتر وبزبسیار و خوب شود.»

"On the west is a large separate territory called Kachcha...(the physical aspect of the country is) barren and sandy. There is an excellent breed of horses believed to be of Arabian race, and there are good camels and goats."

In another place Abu'l-faḍl[13] explains the common belief of his time about the origin of Kachh horses:

«(اسپ های) سرزمین کچّه تازی آسا. چنان برگذارند در پیشین زمان جهازی ازبّر عرب تباهی بآن سرزمین افتاد. هفت اسپ گزین داشت واسپ آن جا را از آن نژاد بر شمارند.»

"(The horses of) Kachcha excel, being equal to Arabs. It is said that a long time ago an Arab ship was wrecked and driven to shore at Kachcha; and that it had seven choice horses, from which, according to the general belief, the breed of that country originated."

Thus the presence of a good breed of horses in Kachh from "a long time ago" may have been the origin of the story in the *Mahābhārata*.

In the second century A.D. Ptolemy[14] mentions the name of a town Bardaxema situated at some distance from the easternmost branch of the Indus on the coast of the Kanthi Gulf. He gives the location as 113° 40′ E. by 19° 40′ N., and shows it in his map as a fortified town on the north-east coast of the Kanthi Gulf. This gulf is widely accepted as being the same as the present Gulf of Kachh, but there are conflicting views on the location of Ptolemy's Bardaxema. J. Burgess[15] suggests that it may be an old site near a small village known today as Bardiyā, which is possibly a reminiscence of the Greek name. This village, however, is not located on the Gulf of Kachh, but on the west coast of Kathiawad or present Surashtra.

H. Yule[16] has a different theory about the location of Bardaxema; he tries to equate the place with Porbandar, a port again on the west coast of Kathiawad and south of the village of Bardiyā. Yule's hypothesis has been criticized by W.F. Sinclair[17] who maintained that Porbandar was a modern port with no historical background. Instead, Sinclair suggested Bhadravāti as a possibility for the site of Bardaxema. This is particularly worthy of attention since apart from the similarity of the names. Bhadravāti, according to Ptolemy, is located on the same spot as Bardaxema.

The site seems also to have been known to the early Islamic scholar Abū Rayhān al-Bīrūnī. In his book on India[18] he mentions Bhadra as the name for three distinct countries. Two of these countries he reports as being located in eastern and northern India, and do not concern us here. The third Bhadra (بَهَدْرَ) however, is recorded along with Kachh (کَچ) as two independent states to the south. In another place[19] al-Bīrūnī explains that Kachh is located to the east of Daybul and on the way to Sūmnāt (سومنات = Somnath). Hence al-Bīrūnī's Bhadra, which is mentioned together with Kachh, is likely to be Bhadravāti. It is interesting

---

[11] J. Talboys Wheeler, *History of India from the Earliest Ages*, I, *Mahā Bhārata*, London, 1867, 382-5; *Mahābhārata*, Skandayuddha, paragraph 506 and 507.

[12] Abu'l-faḍl 'Allāmī b. Shaykh Mubārak Nāgūrī, *'A'īn-i Akbarī*, ed. Blochmann, I, Calcutta, 1882, 492; English translation by H.S. Jarrett, II, Calcutta, 1891, 250.

[13] *Ibid.*, Persian text, 140; English translation by Blochmann, Calcutta, 1873, I, 132.

[14] Ptolemy, Book VII, Chapters 1, 3; J.W. McCrindle ed., *Ancient India as Described by Ptolemy*, London, 1885, 33.

[15] *Ibid.*, 37.

[16] H. Yule, *Historical Atlas of Ancient Geography, Biblical and Classical*, London, 1874, Map of Ancient India.

[17] W.F. Sinclair, Book notes, *Indian Antiquary*, 1875, 283.

[18] Abū Rayhān al-Bīrūnī, *Taḥqīq mā li-al-hind*, ed. E. Sachau, London, 1887, 152, 153 and 155; English translation by H. Sachau, London, 1888, I, 301.

[19] *Ibid.*, Arabic text, 102.

that al-Bīrūnī describes the place as a country and not a city. This statement confirms the information in the *Bantvijaya Chronicle*, which claims that during the ancient and mediaeval periods Bhadravāti was always an independent state.

A change in the name of Bhadravāti took place during the middle ages. The date of the change is recorded in the *Bantvijaya Chronicle* as V.E. 798/A.D. 741, when the king of Bhadravāti was defeated by the Solankis (Chaulukyans), the Rajputs of Bhangadh. As maintained by the chronicle the victorious raja ruled in Bhadravāti for only four years, during which time he changed the name of the place to Bhadreśvar. The village is still called by that name, but the old name is not totally forgotten today, and is still known locally.

The date given in the chronicle is hardly acceptable since, as Burgess has already noted,[20] it is nearly two centuries too early for the Chaulukyan Rajputs. If there is any truth in this version, the event cannot be earlier than the 10th century. This conclusion may be of some help for fixing the beginning of the Islamic settlement in Bhadreśvar.

The *Bantvijaya Chronicle* speaks of the Muslims well before the change of the city's name, and as early as the time of Chaudā Akkad Raja, who is said to have ruled from V.E. 670-747/A.D. 613-690. The chronicle contends that Chaudā Akkad entrusted the government to a Muslim prime minister after he noticed faults in the conduct of his former ministers in state affairs. The merchants of the city soon proved this prime minister's administration to be faulty too. He was put to death and the raja took the government upon himself. The Muslims then became the victims of the raja's hatred, and each day he had one of the members of their community killed. At last the raja's hostility against the Muslims led to a war. First a small invading Muslim force came, but it was shortly followed by an Iranian army under the command of a figure, traditionally known as Sayyid La'l Shāh. Akkad Raja defeated this army and treacherously killed its commander. The *Bantvijaya Chronicle* then maintains that soon two Muslim brothers, who were known as *awlīā'*, conquered the city and from that time Muslim power increased. In V.E. 747/A.D. 690 "one thousand pillared mosques" were built, and around the same time other Islamic structures, including the tomb of La'l Shahbāz, were erected.

The content of this story seems to be no more than distorted memories of some early Indo-Islamic relationship, not always of a friendly nature. Its date is also excessively early since no Arab raid is known to have taken place in India earlier than A.H. 93/A.D. 711-12, when Muḥammad b. al-Qāsim invaded Sind and the province of Multan. Even then there is no evidence to suggest that towns as far eastward as Bhadreśvar were also attacked. Not long after the conquest of Multan, the unfortunate Muḥammad, while organizing an army to march on the Indian mainlands, was put to death by the new Caliph Sulaymān b. 'Abd al-Malik.[21] No other Arab attempt at expansion to the east ever took place.

However, as already mentioned, the dates of the chronicle appear to be at least two centuries too early for this period. The chronicle may indeed reflect some events, but they could have taken place only after the 10th century. There had been several Muslim raids on the district of Kachh, the first being that of Maḥmūd of Ghazna in 416/1025-6. On his return from Somnath Maḥmūd avoided a possible confrontation with the Indian army in North Kathiawad (Surashtra). Instead, he re-directed his army to the district of Kachh. The story is related by the court poet, Farrukhī,[22] who was travelling with the Sultan on this occasion, and says that Maḥmūd passed the Rann of Kachh and led his army through the desert to al-Manṣūra, the capital of Sind. Farrukhī does not mention Bhadreśvar, but other historians have recorded a place called Bhīswāra[23] as having been attacked by Maḥmūd's army. According to Mīr Khwand:[24]

«در این اثناء (فتح بتخانه سومنات) خبر رسید که صاحب بهیسواره که در هنگام توجه سپاه ظفر قرین گریخته بود حالا در قلعه متحصن شده واز اینجا تا آن حصار چهل فرسخ راه باشد. سلطان را هوس تسخیر قلعه پیدا شده بر آن صوب نهضت فرمرد. چون بدان نواحی قلعه رسید قلعهٔ دید که آبی عظیم بر اطراف آن محیط شده. ازغوّاصان دو شخص بد ست آورده از عمق آب استفسار نمودند. ایشان گفتند که از فلان محل عبور ممکن است

[20] J. Burgess, *Memorandum on the Remains at Gumli, Gop, and in Kachh, etc.*, ASWI, Memoirs, III, 1875, 13.

[21] Al-Balādhurī, *Futūḥ al-buldān*, Beirut, 1958, V, 618.

[22] *Dīwān-i Ḥakīm Farrukhī Sīstānī*, ed. M. Dabir Siaqi, Tehran, 1956, 71.

[23] Mīr Khwand, *Rawḍat al-ṣafā*, Tehran, 1853-4, IV, no page number, but under the title ذکر فتح سومنات بدست سلطان محمود; Ghiyath al-dīn b. Humām al-dīn Khwand Mīr, *Habīb al-siyar*, Tehran, 1974, II, 382-3.

[24] *Rawḍat al-ṣafā*, as above.

اما در زمان گذشتن اگر بتموّج در آید همه هلاك شوند. سلطان بعد از استخاره توکل بر عنایت الهـی کرده با لشکریان اسب در آب راند و بسلامت بپای قلعه رسید. صاحب قلعه چون آن حال مشاهده کرد جریده بگریخت و از آن قلعه غنیمت فراوان بدست سپاه اسلام افتاد. اهالی حصار کشته شدند.»

"At this juncture (the conquest of the temple of Somnath) news arrived that the ruler of Bhīswāra, who had fled at the time of the arrival of the victorious army, was now entrenched in the fort (*qal'a*), and from their position to that fortification was a forty-parasang journey. The Sultan conceived a desire to subjugate the fortress. He gave orders for departure in that direction. When he arrived in the vicinity of that fort, he saw a fort with a great expanse of water surrounding it. He apprehended two of the divers (who were in the vicinity), and questioned them closely concerning the depth of the water. The divers said, 'From such and such a place a crossing is possible, but if at the moment of crossing the sea should become agitated everyone will perish'. After taking an omen from the Qur'ān the Sultan placed his reliance on the mercy of God, and drove his horse into the water with the soldiers, and arrived safely at the foot of the castle. The master (*ṣāḥib*) of the fort, when he realized the situation, immediately took flight. From that castle plentiful booty fell into the hands of the army of Islam. The inhabitants of the fortification were put to death".

The similarity of the two names, the location of Bhīswāra, its distance from Somnath, and its situation near the sea leave little doubt that Mīr Khwand's Bhīswāra can only be the same as Bhadreśvar. Therefore it may be assumed that Maḥmūd raided the city on his path from Somnath to al-Manṣūra. It must be noted that at the time of Mīr Khwand, Bhadreśvar had already lost its importance and is unlikely to have been known to him. His passage on Bhīswāra may have been taken from an earlier source, otherwise unattested, most probably the now lost history of Maḥmūd written by his court historian Bayhaqī.

After the departure of Maḥmūd, Bhadreśvar does not seem to have remained under Islamic control, since Mīr Khwand's "master of the fort" is maintained by the *Bantvijaya Chronicle* to be the final winner of the war. It would not have been difficult for him to return to his city, after Maḥmūd's departure, claiming some sort of victory over his enemy's army.

That the city remained under the control of the local Jain ruler is also confirmed by the text of the inscription in the temple of Bhadreśvar dated 10th of Vad, V.E.1195/A.D.1139.[25] It speaks of a grant given by the local Jain ruler for the building of some temples. The date of this inscription is only 20 years earlier than that of the Islamic mausoleum, that is to say, at the time of this inscription the Muslims must have been well established in the city, but without being directly involved in the local conduct of political affairs.

There are further indications showing that during the time of the Islamic settlement, indicated by the dates of the graves as being between 554/1159-60 and 625/1227-8, the city remained in the hands of the local Jains. Several historical sources, to be discussed below, speak of a merchant from Bhadreśvar known as Jagadeva,[26] who ruled in the city during this period. The version of the *Bantvijaya Chronicle* says that in V.E.1182/A.D.1125, the Solanki Raja Noughan handed the government of Bhadreśvar to this merchant. The Raja offered him a charter which transferred to Jagadeva "the absolute right of enjoyment so long as the sun continued to revolve".

Jagadeva is a well known Jain figure and his story has been recorded by many historians of this faith. The earliest account is, however, a work known as the *Jagaducharita*, published by G. Bühler[27] in 1892 and supposed by this scholar to be a work of the second half of the 14th or the beginning of the 15th century. The *Jagaducharita* claims that Bhadreśvar was attacked by Pīṭhadeva, the ruler of Pāra, who took over and occupied the city, and finally destroyed its fortifications. Jagadeva, still at that time a merchant and a shipowner of Bhadreśvar, went to the Chaulukyan king Lavanaprasāda at Anahilapataka with a request for an army to liberate his city. His wish was granted by the king, and when he returned to Bhadreśvar he defeated Pīṭhadeva and himself became the ruler. Pīṭhadeva first fled to some unknown place and soon afterwards died. Thus it appears that the Chaulukyan

---

[25] J. Burgess, *Memorandum on the Antiquities at Dabhoi, Ahmedabad*, etc., ASWI, III, Bombay, 1814, appendix, Bhadreśvar inscriptions, 8, inscription no. 56.

[26] The name in the *Bantvijaya Chronicle* is given as Jagdevaśā, in other sources such as the *Jagaducharita* or the *Panchaśatīprabodhasambandha* (Indian Studies no. 1) the name also appears as Jagadu.

[27] G. Bühler, *The Jagaducharita of Sarvanada*, a historical romance from Gujarat, Indian Studies, no. 1, *Sitzungsberichte*, CXXVI, Wien, 1892.

ruler's generous offer of the governorship of Bhadreśvar to Jagadeva mentioned by the *Bantvijaya Chronicle* was not without political interest. With the help of the army, but mainly by their own efforts, the people of Bhadreśvar could repulse an intruding enemy as well as keep a good relationship with the Bhadreśvar merchants who became the ruling class.

The invading king Pīṭhadeva is identified by Bühler with the Sumra chief Dadu Phitu (or Phatu),[28] a popular and powerful Muslim king of Sind.[29] According to the *Tuḥfat al-kirām*,[30] Phitu ruled between 590/1193-4 and 623/1226. The date of Pīṭhadeva's wars against Bhadreśvar are not given in the *Jagaducharita*. The only date given is that of a famine which afflicted Bhadreśvar in V.E.1312/A.D.1255, some years after the wars. None of the dates in any of these sources is accurate. It can only be assumed that the events must have taken place sometime in the second half of the 12th or early 13th century. This period is of importance for the present study since it embraces the date of all the Islamic remains of Bhadreśvar.

It seems nevertheless unlikely that these remains could be attributable to Pīṭhadeva's short occupation of the city, since their inscribed dates span a period of nearly a century. In such circumstances it is hard to believe that after the subsequent liberation of Bhadreśvar, a Sumra settlement, founded during the occupation, could have continued to survive. It has to be assumed, therefore, that the Muslim community of the city had stood aloof from political events, and did not depend directly on the state of Sind. We shall shortly attempt to investigate this Muslim community in greater detail, but first the other events of the reign of Jagadeva have to be noted.

The *Jagaducharita* maintains that after Pīṭhadeva's defeat Jagadeva was involved with an extensive reconstruction of the city which had been left in ruins by the enemy. The *Bantvijaya Chronicle* also notes that the merchant ruler repaired the temple on a large scale, removing all traces of antiquity. Burgess[31] reports that in the temple on several of the columns are inscriptions dated V.E. 1223/A.D. 1166 to V.E. 1235/ A.D. 1178. Furthermore, in the shrine there are images of Parśvanātha and Sāntinātha both dated V.E. 1232/A.D. 1175. The inscriptions, according to Burgess, note that the stones on which they were written were votive offerings by individuals, made while the temple was being rebuilt. These dates also correspond with the date of the reconstruction given in the *Bantvijaya Chronicle*.

According to the *Jagaducharita*, during the reconstruction of the city Jagadeva also built a mosque (*masīti*) for the *Shimalī* "by reason of the wealth of the *mlechchhas*". According to Bühler,[32] the word Shimalī probably indicates the Ismā'īlīs. He does not give a precise meaning for the word *mlechchha* apart from a general meaning of foreigner, but in this particular case the word evidently seems to indicate the Arabs, or the merchants from the Persian Gulf region[33]. Thus the quotation from the *Jagaducharita* identifies the sect of the Muslims settled at Bhadreśvar, and also indicates that the mosque was built with the help of the local Jains. Presumably it would refer to the main mosque of Bhadreśvar, and if the date of V.E. 1223/A.D. 1166 is accepted for the beginning of its construction this would have been only six years later than the date of the inscription in the mausoleum.

Jagadeva's governorship appears from the *Jagaducharita* to have remained under the suzerainty of the Chaulukyans of Gujarat. He continued his struggle with the Muslim rulers, or as they are designated in this chronicle, the *mudgalas*.[34] Bühler explains that in the Jain chronicles of the 14th century onwards this word is used not only for the Mughals or Mongols but is also generalized to include any Muslims. The same expression is also used in the *Bantvijaya Chronicle*[35] where it speaks of Akkad Raja's war against the Muslim armies.

The Indian scholar Ashoke Kumar Majumdar[36] suggests that the reference to the Mudgalas in the *Jagaducharita* may be an allusion to the campaigns in A.D. 1224 by Jalāl al-dīn Mangubistī Khwārazmshāh who sent an army under Khāṣ Khān to pillage Naharwāla. Apart from the late date of this event the

[28] *Ibid.*, 31.

[29] Sayyid Muḥammad Ma'ṣūm Bakkarī, *Tārīkh-i Sind*, Poona, 1938, 61, 290.

[30] Mīr 'Alī Shīr Qāni' Thathawī, *Tuḥfat al-kirām*, Hyderabad, 1971, 69; Urdu translation by Akhtar Razawi, Karachi, 1959, 124.

[31] J. Burgess, *Report on the Antiquities of Kaṭhiawād and Kachh*, 1874-5, ASWI, II, 1876, 207-8; Inscriptions at Bhadreśvar, *Memorandum on the Antiquities at Dabhoi, Ahmadabad, etc.*, ASWI, III, 1875, appendix, 10-14.

[32] *The Jagaducharita of Sarvanada*, 18.

[33] James Todd, *Annals and Antiquities of Rajasthan*, I, Calcutta, 1899, 256-60.

[34] *The Jagaducharita of Sarvanada*, 19.

[35] J. Burgess, *Memorandum on the Remains at Gumli, Gop, and in Kachh, etc.*, ASWI, Memoirs, III, 1875, 13.

[36] A.K. Majumdar, *Chalukyans of Gujarat*, Bombay, 1956, 160.

earliest detailed history referring to Jalāl al-dīn's campaign is the *Tārīkh-i Juwaynī*,[37] but from its text it does not make it clear how far and in which direction Khāṣ Khān led his army. Thus it is more likely that the *Jagaducharita* was referring to some local battles between the Sumras and the Chaulukyans other than the one involving Pīṭhadeva which is already mentioned. It should be borne in mind that the Sumras themselves were originally from Kachh[38] and were in a state of continuous struggle with the Chaulukyans in this region.

At first glance the existence of an Islamic settlement in Bhadreśvar during a period of war between the city and the Muslim armies seems to be strange. It is even more strange to find the settlement under the protection of an Indian government. However, it must be noted that Bhadreśvar was a commercial centre with an important and influential merchant community. The interests of the rulers would have been served by the maintenance of their commercial ties with the Muslims in the lands to the west. This would have led to a desire to extend their links with the Ismā'īlī community.

A bilingual inscription found in the vicinity of Somnath in Gujarat, and its Sanskrit version kept in the temple of Harsayā in Veraval,[39] show that the Islamic settlement of Bhadreśvar was by no means an exceptional case. This inscription refers to another Muslim community living in Somnath, and is dated both to the Ḥijra year 662 and V.E. 1320/A.D. 1263. The Sanskrit version refers to the Prophet Muḥammad as "the teacher of the sailors who live near the holy temple of Viśvaratha". Such a reference indicates particularly that the commercial communities of Muslims in India were trying to communicate with the local people in understandable and acceptable terms. In other towns of Gujarat evidence of the existence of other Muslim communities has also been found, including some dated tombstones and the mosque of Abulqāsim b. 'Alī al-Īrajī, described in the appendix.

The existence of Muslim settlements in many cities of India is also recorded in many early Muslim geographies, one of the earliest records being that of the *Ḥudūd al-'Ālam*[40] written in 372/982-3 and mentioning four cities: Ṣimūr, Sindān, Sūbāra, and Kanbāya, all with Muslim communities having their own *jāmi'* mosques. Kanbāya is the same as modern Cambay in Gujarat, but the other towns cannot be precisely identified. Istakhrī[41] also records the same information adding to the list another town, Qāmuhul. Al-Idrīsī[42] records two other towns:

«ومن بلاد الهند المضمنة فى هذا الجزء خابيرون و أساول و
هما مدينتان عامرتان بالناس و التجّار و الفعلة وأموالهم وافرة و
صنعهم حسنة و بضاعاتهم نافقة. وقد وصل المسلمون الى أكثر
هذه البلاد و تغلبوا على أطرافها فى هذا الوقت و سنذكر ما اتصل
بهذه البلاد من غيرها بحول الله و قوته.»

"Of the land of India included in this section are Khābīrūn and Asāwul, and they are two cities well provided with population and merchants and labourers. Their wealth is plentiful, their industries are admirable, and their merchandise is remunerative. The Muslims came to most parts of the country, and gained possession of parts of it at this time, and we shall relate what adjoins it other than these with God's aid and strength".

The people of many of these settlements appear to have been of the Ismā'īlī sect. According to Professor Abbas Husain al-Hamdani,[43] who has studied the Ismā'īlī manuscripts closely, the Musta'liyān Da'wā of Yemen were in contact with the Muslims of Gujarat from 460/1067-8 until 944/1537-8, during which time they exercised a thorough Arab influence. It may be concluded, therefore, that the Ismā'īlī settlement of

---

[37] 'Atā Malik b. Muḥammad al-Juwaynī, *Tārīkh-i jahān gushā*, II, Leiden, 1916, 148; also see Abū 'Umar Minhāj al-dīn 'Uthmān b. Sirāj al-dīn Jawzjānī, *Ṭabaqāt-i Nāṣirī*, ed. A.H. Habibi, Kabul, 1963, I, 316; Khwand Mīr, *Tārīkh-i ḥabīb al-sīyar*, Tehran, 1974, II, 658-60. These sources record the name of the sultan as Jalāl al-dīn Minkubarnī or Mīnkubarnī. For the details of the events also see: *Sīrat-i Jalāloddin, Story of the Last Khwārazmshāh*, ed. Mojtaba Minovi, Tehran, 1965, 114-122. This source does not mention Khāṣ Khān, but records one Jahān Pahlawān Uzbik who was left in "Hind" by Jalāl al-dīn, and was forced to escape to Iran in 727/1326-7.

[38] Sayyid Muḥammad Ma'ṣūm Bakkarī, *Tārīkh-i Sind*. Poona, 1938, 61.

[39] E. Hultzsch, A grant of Arjunada of Gujarat, *Indian Antiquary*, XI, 1882, 241-5; for the Arabic version of the inscription see Z.A. Desai, Arabic Inscriptions of the Rajput period from Gujarat, *Epigraphia Indica, Arabic and Persian Supplement*, 1961, 10-15.

[40] *Ḥudūd al-'ālam min al-mashriq ilā al-maghrib*, ed. M. Sotoodeh, Tehran, 1962, 66.

[41] Abū Isḥāq Ibrāhīm b. Muḥammad al-Istakhrī, *al-Masālik wa al-mamālik* (Arabic text), Cairo, 1961, 102, 104-5; *Masālik wa Mamālik* (Persian translation of 5th or 6th/11th or 12th century), ed. I. Afshar, Tehran, 1961, 147, 151. Istakhrī records the name of one of the towns as Ṣaymūr and not Ṣimūr as given by the *Ḥudūd al-'ālam*.

[42] Abū 'Abdullāh Muḥammad b. Muḥammad al-Idrīsī, *Opus Geographicum*, Napoli-Roma, 1971, 185.

[43] Abbas Husain al-Hamdani, *Ismā'īlī Da'wā: The Beginning of the Ismā'īlī Da'wā in Northern India*, Cairo, 1956, 15.

Bhadreśvar was one among many, with a mixed population from different parts of the Islamic world, and probably linked to one of the Ismā'īlī states, but not directly connected with the Muslims of Sind, who were, incidentally, followers of the same sect during the 12th and 13th centuries.

The final fate of the Islamic settlement of Bhadreśvar remains uncertain, but is unlikely to have been very different from the unfortunate destiny of the city itself. The latest Islamic inscription of Bhadreśvar is on a tombstone dated 624/1227. As appears from several Indian chronicles such as Kathevate's *Kīrti-kaumudī*[44] and the *Parabandha-kośa*,[45] in V.E. 1288/A.D. 1231, or shortly after, Viradhvala, the ruler of Dholka, made war against Bhīmasinha of Bhadreśvar. At first he was unsuccessful, but later he returned with a strong force and occupied the city. After these wars Bhadreśvar lost its importance. The *Bantvijaya Chronicle* maintains that after V.E. 1506/A.D. 1449, when Bhuj became the centre of power, the true decline of Bhadreśvar began. Finally in V.E. 1817/A.D. 1760 the court of Bhuj gave orders for the dismantling of the remains of the city walls and the main buildings of Bhadreśvar, thereby reducing it to a small village.

There is no evidence to show what happened at this time to the Muslim settlement there. In 1896 the existence of a small group of Ismā'īlīs in the village of Bhadreśvar was reported by Dalpatram Khakhar.[46] Today some Isma'īlīs still live in the village. During his visit to the site the present writer met two persons from the community, but found them to be unaware of the historical traditions discussed here, and lacking information on the origin of their community and monuments. The writer was told by others that they do not have any mosque in the village. In the case of the tombs they had no knowledge of their origin, but instead passed on the legendary accounts which will be discussed in a later chapter.

THE SITE OF ANCIENT BHADREŚVAR AND THE SHRINE OF IBRĀHĪM

Ancient Bhadreśvar is over one kilometre north of the coast and extends over an area of more than 1500m. by 900m. (fig. 2, pl. 1). The continuous outline of the fortifications can no longer be traced above the present ground level, but a small section of ruined wall still stands at the eastern side of the site, which may be part of the old circumvallation. As mentioned earlier, the *Bantvijaya Chronicle* claims that the stones of the city wall, together with those of certain large buildings, were taken away as late as V.E. 1817/A.D. 1760. Burgess[47] also reports that the demolition continued until 1810, when even the old temples were dismantled and the stones taken to Mundra to build a new port. Nonetheless, many large blocks of stone which have not been used are still lying scattered over the site.

The Ancient Site

The present village of Bhadreśvar occupies part of the western side of the site, and it is not easy to say whether or not the village falls within the original perimeter. Many buildings in this village are in fact made from the stones of older structures, and some of these reused stones still show fragments of elaborate carvings. The great Jain temple, known as the Vasai temple, stands about 200m. further to the east. This temple is now surrounded by modern structures serving as residential quarters, guest houses and shops. All these buildings are enclosed by a relatively modern wall, forming a compound with two entrances. The main entrance is on the western side of this modern enclosure and there is a secondary entrance to the north. Outside the northern entrance is an old well, the circular shaft of which is lined with large blocks of stone. On the western side of the shaft, and immediately below ground level, there is a niche recessed into the side of the well, and lined with similar stones, but decorated with simple carvings. Traces of the winch-fittings can still be seen at the front of the niche, and indicate that the niche would have been used as a vantage point from where water was drawn. However, no means of access to the niche from ground level now survives, and any that may have once existed

[44] The writer did not have access to this source, but the information is taken from Gulab Chandra Chaudhary, *Political History of Northern India from Jain Sources*, Amritsar, 1954, 304.

[45] *Rajaśekhara Suri*, ed. Jina Vijaya, Ahmadabad, 1935, 104.

[46] Dalpatram Khakhar, Castes and tribes in Kachh, *The Indian Antiquary*, Bombay, 1876, 71.

[47] J. Burgess, *Report on the Antiquities of Kaṭhiawād and Kachh*, 1874-5, ASWI, II, 1876, 208.

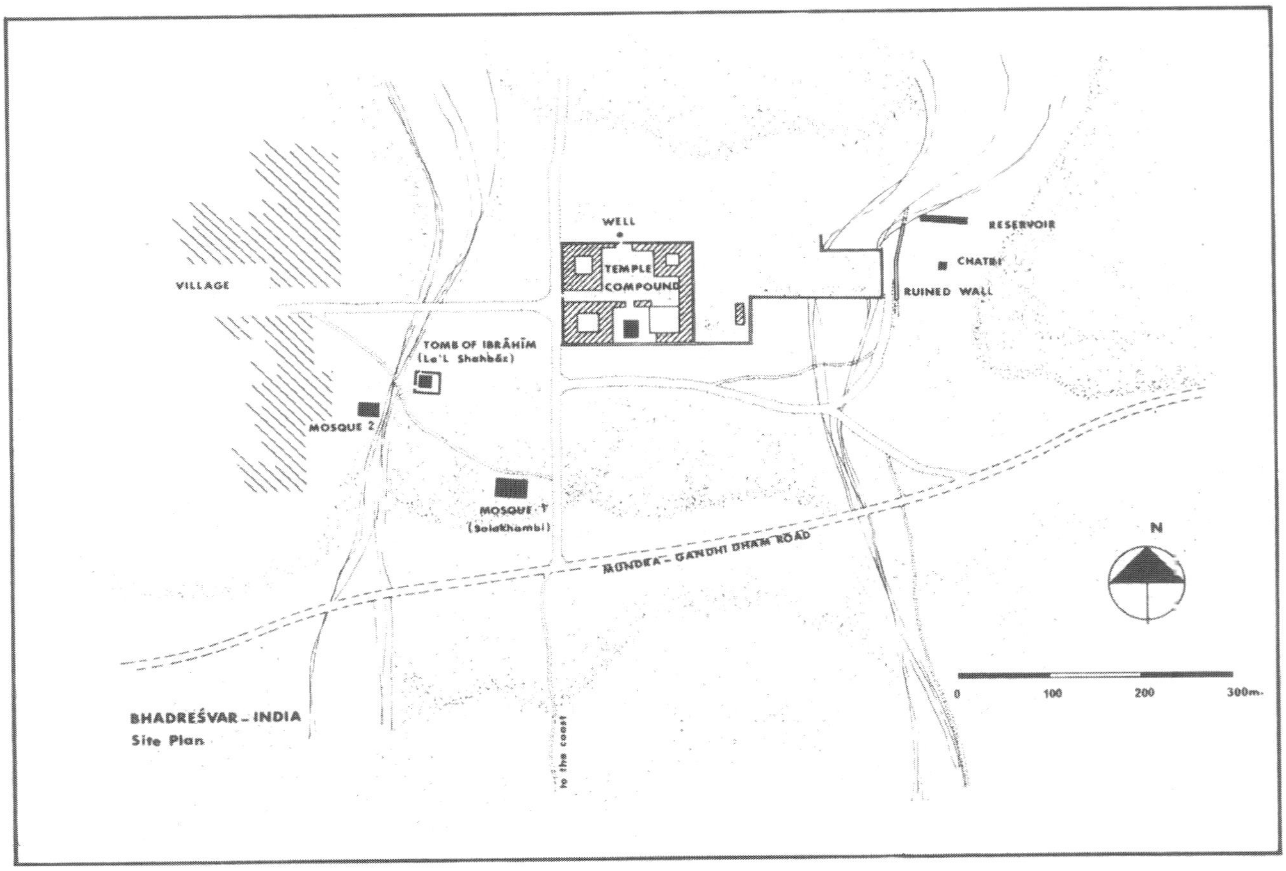

Fig. 2 Sketch plan of the ancient site of Bhadreśvar.

must have been removed without leaving any trace, nor are any remains of a superstructure visible around the well. While water is still to be seen in the shaft, it was said by local people that the well is no longer in everyday use.

The traces of ancient walling, which perhaps represent part of the former circumvallation, are located some 300m. to the east of the temple compound, and close to a modern wall which protects certain agricultural land belonging to the temple. A track now passes through the remains both of the old circumvallation and the modern wall. The ancient works are built with large blocks of stone laid without mortar. This ashlar construction is characteristic of the old buildings of Bhadreśvar, and is indeed a well-known method in ancient Gujarat, as of course in many other parts of India. We have noted that today very little of this perimeter stands above ground level. The present remains run from south to north for about 70m. and then change direction somewhat towards the north-east for another 50m. ("ruined wall" on fig. 2). Beyond this point the stone blocks of the line of the wall are no longer visible *in situ* at ground level, but in both directions the alignment is traceable as a bank of earth some 50cm. high. As for the original function of this circumvallation, it is at present uncertain whether it was merely to protect the temple area, or to serve as a fortification of the city as a whole, but its substantial length and massive structure suggest that it may be part of the original city wall.

The dated Islamic shrine and the two mosques of Bhadreśvar are located at the south-western edge of the site, between the village and the temple. There are also two other ancient structures in Bhadreśvar: a pavilion dome of the type known in Indian architecture as a chatri, and the remains of a *wāv* or "well-

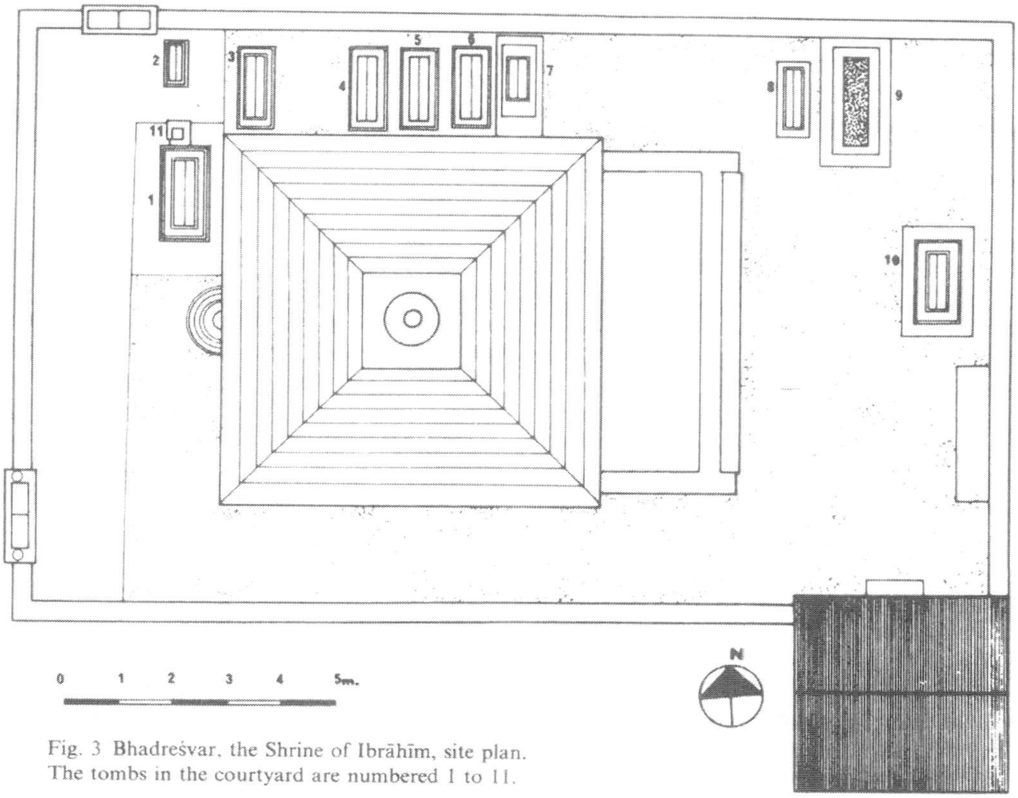

Fig. 3 Bhadreśvar, the Shrine of Ibrāhīm, site plan. The tombs in the courtyard are numbered 1 to 11.

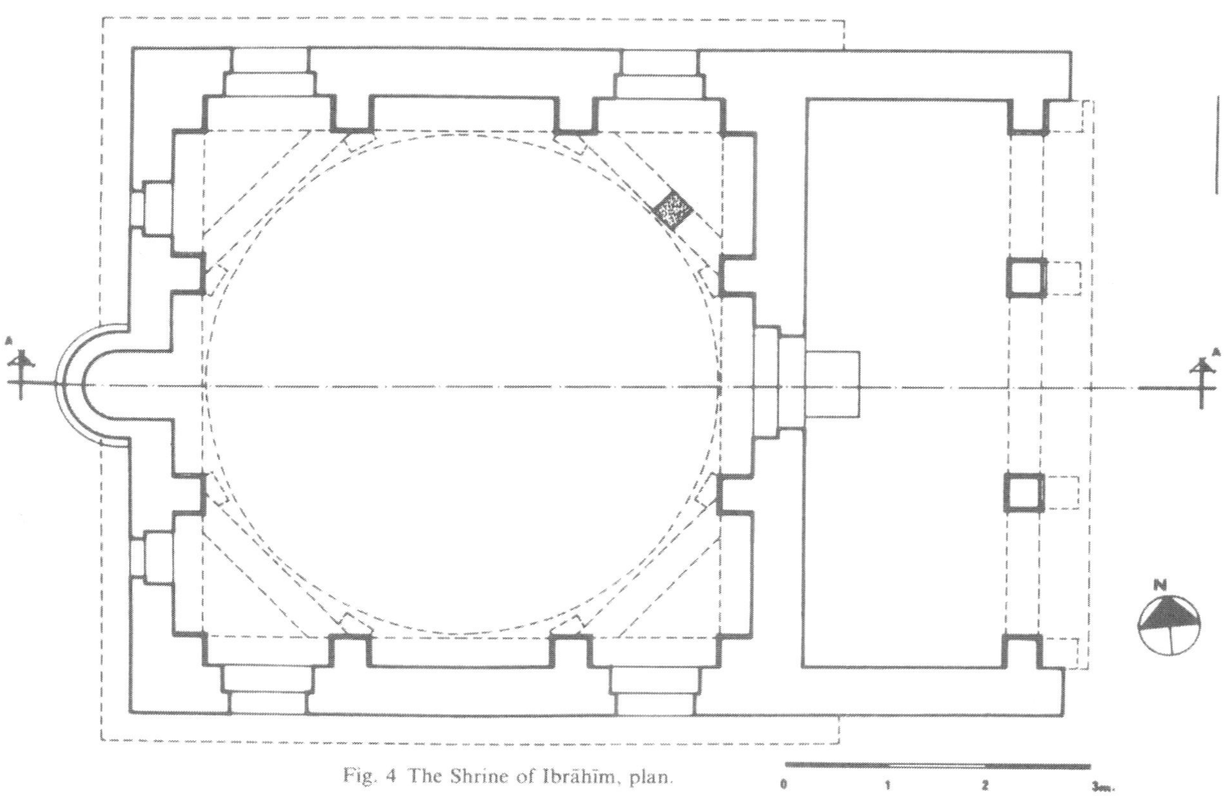

Fig. 4 The Shrine of Ibrāhīm, plan.

reservoir", locally known as the Dūdhā Wāv. All of these structures will be studied in detail below.

The Shrine of Ibrāhīm

The only dated Islamic monument of Bhadreśvar, the Shrine of Ibrāhīm (Dargāh La'l Shahbāz) (figs. 3-9, pls. 2-11), is situated 140m. outside the south-west corner of the temple compound. The shrine bears an inscription dated *dhi'l-hijja* 554/December 1159-January 1160, the earliest Islamic date, seen *in situ*, on any Islamic monument in India (fig. 42, pls. 43-5). The inscription will be discussed in Part Two by Manijeh Bayani-Wolpert. The building is regarded by the local Muslim community as a holy shrine. While the name of one Ibrāhīm is mentioned in the inscription, it is now attributed by the local inhabitants to a personage known as La'l Shahbāz, a well-known legendary figure among the Shi'ites of Sind and Gujarat.

Events in the life of La'l Shahbāz are recorded in several histories of Sind such as the *Tārīkh-i Sind*[48] and the *Tuḥfat al-kirām*.[49] According to the latter, Makhdūm La'l Shahbāz was the nickname of Shaykh 'Uthmān Marwandī, a descendant of the Shi'ite Imām Ja'far al-Ṣādiq, who in 662/1263-4 went from Sind to Multan, to the court of Sultan Muḥammad, son of Sultan Ghiyāth al-dīn Balban. Later, however, he returned to Sind and settled in Sehwan, where he finally died in 673/1274-5. Since that time his tomb in Sehwan has been regarded as one of the holiest shrines in Sind. In 1929 Henry Cousens[50] published a report on Sehwan in which he studied this shrine in detail. It is clear that the attribution of the Shrine of Ibrāhīm at Bhadreśvar to La'l Shahbāz is merely traditional and has no historical value.

The shrine is now situated in a courtyard enclosed by a relatively modern wall, many stones of which are taken from older buildings (fig. 3, pl. 2a). The building itself consists of a square chamber with a portico in front of the entrance at the eastern side (figs. 4-8). The chamber measures 5.70 × 5.70m. across the interior and the portico 5.70 × 1.98m. The walls are 48cm. in thickness. At present there are no traces of a grave inside the chamber or in the portico, but in the courtyard there are graves of different personages which will be discussed later.

The structure is built with large blocks of stone, evenly cut and laid without mortar. The flat roof of the portico is supported at the eastern side by two columns, and there are two pilasters of corresponding form on the inner faces of its projecting walls (pls. 2b and 3a). The chamber is roofed by a dome, pyramidal on the exterior and conical within. There are no columns in the interior of the chamber. The dome is supported on twelve pilasters similar to those of the portico, by means of stone brackets in the form of ante-capitals decorated with foliations, and above them monolithic lintels (pls. 8 and 9). The shafts of the columns of the portico and also the pilasters are monolithic but stand on separate square bases decorated with triangular floral motifs. Decorative carvings divide each shaft into three different registers. In the case of the columns the lower register is square, the middle octagonal, and the upper circular and more elaborately ornamented than the other parts. Around the neck of the shaft runs a course of "pot and foliage" motifs (pls. 4b and 6a). Below the foliage are carved vertical strings of beads, and further down a horizontal collar of diamonds alternating with discs which overpass the ends of the vertical strings. Similar motifs are used on the pilasters, but in this case all the three registers of the shafts are square in plan, being distinguished merely by their mouldings.

The decorative motifs used on the columns and the pilasters of the Shrine of Ibrāhīm are similar to those traditionally used in Jain architecture. Analogies can be seen at many sites such as the Luna Vasahi temple at Mount Abu[51] and the Neminatha temple in Kumhari,[52] both built during the 12th century. In the mosque of Arhāī din kā Jhonpra at Ajmer similar Jain columns have been reused.[53] There is also decoration of this kind in the temple of Bhadreśvar itself.[54]

---

[48] Sayyid Muḥammad Ma'ṣūm Bakkarī, *Tārīkh-i Sind*, Poona 1938, 40.

[49] Mīr 'Alī Shīr Qāni' Thathawī, *Tuḥfat al-kirām*, Urdu tr., Karachi, 1959, 428-30.

[50] H. Cousens, *The Antiquities of Sind*, ASI, Imperial Series, XLVI, Calcutta, 1929, 140.

[51] A. Gosch, ed., *Jaina Art and Architecture*, II, New Delhi, 1975, 191-2, pl. 188.

[52] *Ibid.*, pl. 189.

[53] *Ibid.*, 249, pl. 147.

[54] J. Burgess, *Report on the Antiquities of Kaṭhiawād and Kachh*, 1874-5, ASWI, II, 1876, pl. 60.

Fig. 5 The Shrine of Ibrāhīm, section A-A.

The portico has a flat ceiling (pl. 7a) made up of ten slabs, one of which is now missing. It was originally decorated with 27 squares, arranged in nine rows of three, each having a lotus motif in the middle. Similar lotus motifs can also be seen on the underside of the lintels of the portico (pl. 6b).

The dated inscription, already mentioned, forms a frieze around the interior of the portico. Burgess speaks of this feature as an architrave, but this is not strictly correct since the architrave is the main load-bearing beam resting on the columns, and in normal architectural practice would not carry major decoration. In the present case the inscription actually forms a frieze all around the walls just under the ceiling. Immediately below the inscription runs a decorative band ornamented with a serpentine garland motif. At the northern side of the portico this motif gives way to an extra line of script containing the end of the inscription.

The entrance to the chamber of the shrine is situated under the portico in the centre of the eastern wall. On the exterior, the jambs and the lintel of the entrance are decorated with garland and "diamond and disc" motifs and, within the rebate, a course of lotus leaf foliation (pl. 3b). All these motifs are characteristically Indian and more precisely Gujarati. Above the entrance, in the middle of the lintel is carved a single diamond framed in a square. While this decoration is entirely Indian in character, the corresponding space in Hindu and Jain temples is usually decorated with images.

Opposite the entrance is the *miḥrāb* (fig. 9, pl. 8). It has the form of a stilted semi-circular recess in the middle of the *qibla* wall, projecting on the exterior beyond the wall line. This *miḥrāb* is plain and shows no traces of decoration. Above the *miḥrāb*, the arch is also semi-circular, a form unusual in pre-Islamic Indian architecture, but already present in Islam, especially further west, in Egypt, where it can be seen at the mosque of al-Azhar[55] dated 361/971-2, and in the madrasa of Qalā'ūn[56] (684/1285-6). As the *miḥrāb* of the Shrine of Ibrāhīm is undecorated it may be as-

[55] K.A.C. Creswell, *The Muslim Architecture of Egypt*, I, Oxford, 1952, pl. 114, d.

[56] *Ibid.*, II, 1959, pl. 108b and c.

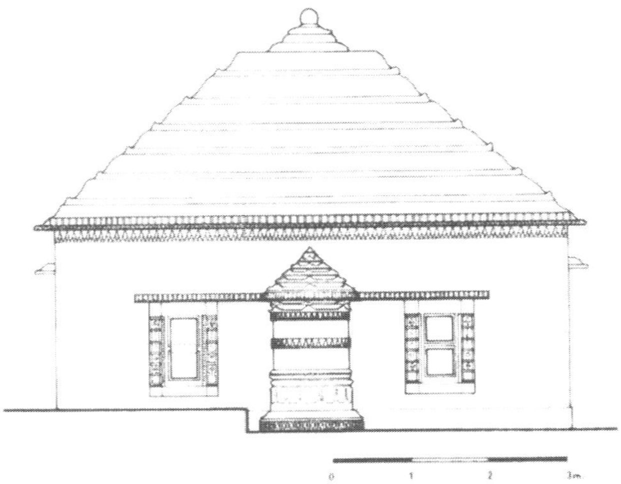

Fig. 6 The Shrine of Ibrāhīm, west elevation.

Fig. 7 The Shrine of Ibrāhīm, east elevation.

sumed to have once been covered with another decorative medium. Around the springing of the *miḥrāb* arch there are two projecting mouldings. These mouldings may have functioned as a slot into which the decoration of the *miḥrāb* could have been fitted. No traces remain of a medium such as plaster; and the form of the slot suggests that a hard material, most probably wood, may have been carved and fitted into the appropriate recess. Thus the decoration of the *miḥrāb* could have been executed elsewhere and imported to Bhadreśvar. Wooden *miḥrābs* of such a type are already known in many parts of the Islamic world, from Afghanistan[57] to Iran[58] and Egypt. Egyptian *miḥrābs* such as those of the mosque of al-Azhar[59] (dated 519/1125-6), the mausoleum of Sayida Nafīsa[60] (c. 532/1137-8) and the mosque of Sayida Ruqīya[61] (c. 549/1154-5) are all of the type assumed: that is to say, semi-circular in plan and pre-fabricated to fit a space provided in the wall.

The *miḥrāb* projects beyond the exterior *qibla* wall (pl. 7b). This method of construction is part of the western Muslim tradition, for example at the Umayyad mosques of Khān al-Zibīb[62] and Jabal Says.[63] Later the same arrangement can be found in the Ayyubid tomb of Abū Manṣūr Ibrāhīm in Egypt.[64] In Iran and Central Asia *miḥrābs* with a semi-circular plan are rare, particularly those which have a projection on the exterior of the wall, as Iranian *miḥrābs* are angular and do not project outside the walls. The only exceptions are in the Abbasid mosques of Ḥājī Piyāda[65] in Balkh, and at Darra-yi Shākh,[66] both in

---

[57] *Miḥrāb* at Charkh; A. Bombaci, Summary report on Italian Archaeological Mission in Afghanistan, *East and West*, X, 1 and 2, 1959, 16, figs. 13 and 14; Souren Melikian-Chirvani, Un chef d'œuvre inconnu dans une vallée afghane, *Connaissance des Arts*, CCCVIII, Oct. 1977; Klaus Fischer, From the rise of Islam to the Mongol Invasion, *The Archaeology of Afghanistan*, ed. F.R. Allchin and N. Hammond, London, 1978, 313.

[58] *Miḥrāb* of the Jāmi' mosque at Ābyāna; R. Ettinghausen, The "Bevelled Style" in the Post-Sammarra Period, *Herzfeld Memorial Volume*, 1948, 77, pl. 12.

[59] Jean David Weill, Les Bois a épigraphes jusqu'à l'époque Mamlouke, *Catalogue du musée arabe*, Cairo, 1931, 5, pl. 12.

[60] *Ibid.*, 4, pl. 14.

[61] *Ibid.*, 11, pl. 16.

[62] K.A.C. Creswell, *Early Muslim Architecture*, I, Oxford, 1932, 287.

[63] *Ibid.*, I, part 2, 1969, 476.

[64] K.A.C. Creswell, *The Muslim Architecture of Egypt*, II, Oxford, 1959, 78.

[65] Galina A. Pugachenkova, Les monuments peu connus de l'architecture médiévale de l'Afghanistan, *Afghanistan*, XXI, 1, 1968, 17-52; Lisa Golombek, Abbasid mosque at Balkh, *Oriental Art*, XV, 1969, 173-189; Asadoulla Souren Melikian-Chirvani, La plus ancienne mosquée de Balkh, *Arts Asiatiques*, XX, 1969, 3-20.

[66] Ralph Pinder-Wilson, Le mihrab decoré de Darra-i Shākh/Gorzivan, *Studia Iranica*, IX, 1, 1980, 90-8.

Afghanistan, the mosque of ʿAlī Shāh in Tabriz[67] and the Gunbad-i ʿAlawyān in Hamadan.[68] The *miḥrāb* of the Gunbad-i ʿAlawyān may, however, be a later addition. On the Iranian coast of the Persian Gulf, where the Arab and Iranian traditions were amalgamated, the *miḥrāb* of the Jāmiʿ Mosque of Sīrāf[69] also projects outside the wall, but is rectangular in plan.

The appearance of the form at Bhadreśvar, therefore, supports the historical indications of a direct link between the Arab lands and the Muslim community of Bhadreśvar. On the exterior projection of the *miḥrāb* of the Shrine of Ibrāhīm there are diamond patterns of the Indian type already mentioned. Furthermore, on the edges of the stepped conical roof of the *miḥrāb* there are ornamental antefixae, a form of the Indian motif used in the decoration of most temples. While the concept of a shrine with a *miḥrāb* is obviously Islamic, details of the work suggest that the craftsmen were Indians. It is interesting that the practice of making the *miḥrābs* project from the exterior wall has survived in India and is now regarded as characteristic of Indian architecture.

On either side of the *miḥrāb* there is a window, again decorated with lotus and diamond motifs (pl. 7b). The chamber has four other larger windows, two in each of the flanking walls, with decorations similar to those of the entrance frame (pls. 4a, 5 and 11b). Above the two windows near the western end are Quranic inscriptions in Kufic style calligraphy (pl. 5). These texts are discussed in Part Two.

The shrine is roofed with a dome of the type known as a corbelled dome, a practice known in Indian architecture from earlier periods. In this method stones are laid horizontally with each of the courses overlapping the one below. The interior of the dome of this shrine is decorated with lotus segments and lotus-leaf borders (pl. 10). Both the general form of the ceiling and the details are known in Hindu and Jain architecture from previous periods. Amongst many examples, the temples of Mount Abu[70] and the temple of Kaithabeśvara in Annavati[71] provide close analogies to the ceiling of our shrine. The exposed roof of the chamber, as viewed from the exterior, presents the form of a stepped pyramid. This type of roofing is not commonly used in Indian architecture, but already occurs as far east as Bhubaneśvar, on the temples of Brahmeśvara,[72] Megheśvara[73] and Ananta-Vasudeva,[74] all of which are believed to have been erected during the 11th and 12th centuries. At the Shrine of Ibrāhīm the only roof decorations are again the Indian type antefixae, similar to those of the *miḥrāb*, applied on the edge of the roof courses. Below the roof the exterior walls of the chamber are once more decorated with a course of half diamonds and leaf mouldings (figs. 6 and 8, pls. 4a, 5, 7b, and 11).

The other tombs (fig. 3, pl. 11) situated in the courtyard of the shrine have been briefly mentioned. Three of these, numbers 1, 9 and 10 in the plan, are stone sarcophagi, and the rest ordinary graves surmonted by tomb-slabs. The sarcophagus at the northeastern corner of the courtyard (no. 9) is now open and its cover is missing. The remaining tombs are all similar in type, and are covered by two or more slabs superimposed in a stepped pyramidal formation. On the top of these slabs is the usual horizontal gabled gravestone. Except for sarcophagus no. 1, the rest of the tombs are covered with slabs of soft sandstone. Over the centuries their outer layer has been eroded and little survives of their inscriptions and decorations. The best preserved sarcophagus (no. 1) bears a Quranic inscription. Another line of inscription below the Quranic text is badly damaged and obscured with whitewash, but may contain the date. If this were the case, it would follow that the next element described would be from a different monument. This is the inscribed *stele* (no. 11) standing near the head of the sarcophagus. It is square in horizontal section and, as discussed in Part Two, is dated 20th *shaʿbān* 569/26th March 1174. The date is in fact only fifteen years later than that of the shrine, which indicates that it belongs to the early settlement of Bhadreśvar. Its vertical form is not unusual in the Islamic world, since numerous burial *stelae* are found in North Africa.[75] While most are circular in horizontal section and many have been

---

67 A.U. Pope, *A Survey of Persian Art*, London, 1964-5, III, 1057.

68 *Ibid.*, 1020.

69 David Whitehouse, Excavations at Sīrāf, second interim report, *Iran*, VII, 1969, 42, fig. 2.

70 A. Ghosh, ed., *Jaina Art and Architecture*, II, New Delhi, 1975, 301, pls. 183 and 190.

71 H. Cousens, *The Chalukyan Architecture*, ASI, Imperial Series, XLII, 97, pl. 99.

72 Debala Mitra, *Bhubaneśvar*, New Delhi, 1961, 48, pl. 14.

73 *Ibid.*, 56, pl. 20a.

74 *Ibid.*, 57, pl. 20b.

75 Gaston Wiet, Stèles funéraires, *Catalogue général du musée arabe du Caire*, 1939; Mustapha El-Habib, Stèles funéraires kairouanaises du IIIᵉ/IXᵉ au Vᵉ/XIᵉ siècles, *Revue des études islamiques*, XLIII, 1975.

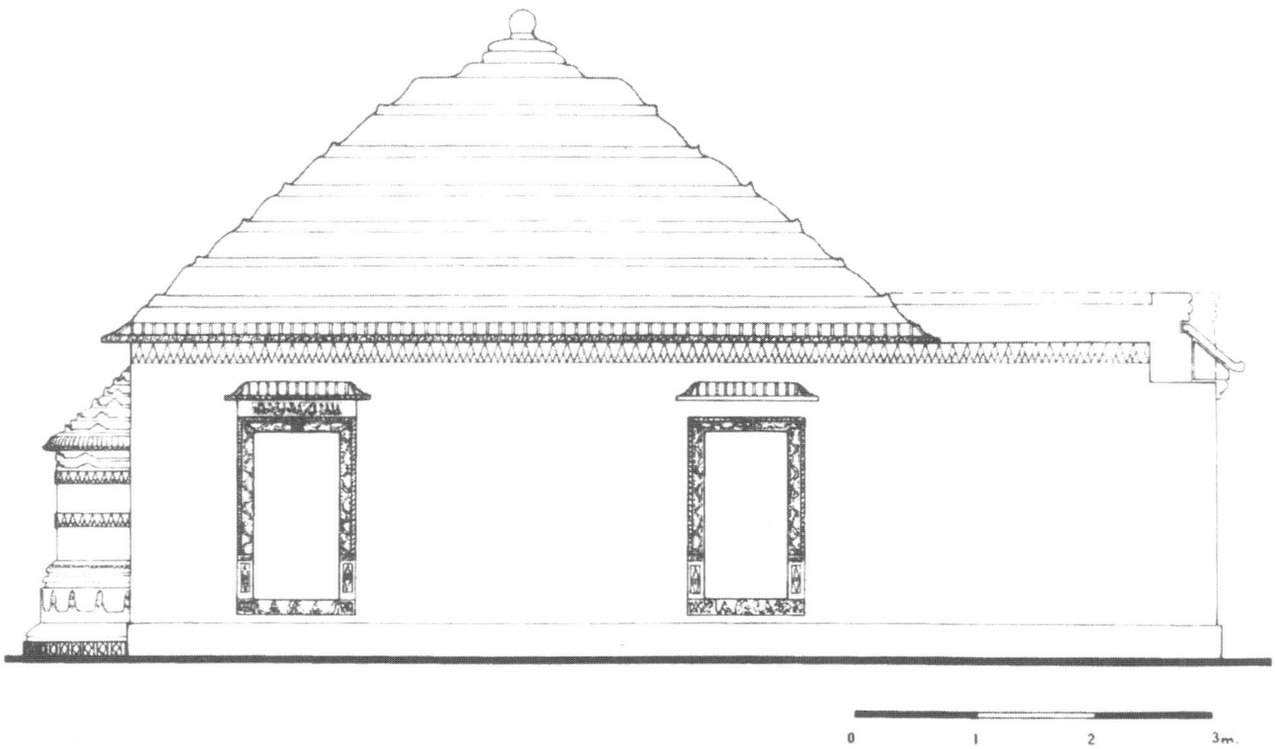

Fig. 8 The Shrine of Ibrāhīm, south elevation.

inspired by classical columns, some examples of angular sections have also been found in Egypt, at the graveyard known as "Ḥosh of the Abbasid Khalifs".[76]

No other date is visible on the tombs inside the courtyard of the Shrine of Ibrāhīm. However, outside the shrine and near the ruins of the larger mosque there are three other graves dating between A.D. 1177 and 1228 as described in Part Two. The tombstones of these graves are similar to those of the courtyard of the shrine and are therefore to be ascribed to the same period. In general form the tombstones resemble Ghaznavid monuments such as that of Sabuktagīn (d. 387/997-8),[77] or of As'ad b. 'Alī[78] datable to the 12th century. At the same time tombstones of similar style must have been widely diffused during this period since examples have also been found at Sīrāf[79] and in North Africa.[80]

A monumental tradition related to that of Bhadreśvar survives in the Chaukhaṇḍi tombs of southern Sind and certain examples in western Gujarat. Many tombs of this style have been studied by Salome Zajadacz-Hastenrath[81] who dates the oldest tomb not earlier than the 15th century. The present writer has also found tombstones of a similar type in an old graveyard in Nagaur in Rajasthan.[82] One of the tombstones is dated *ṣafar* 545/ June 1150 and belongs to one Dūst-'Alī Taqī, son of an Ismā'īlī Dā'ī. This tombstone appears to be connected with another Ismā'īlī community of the mid-12th century in Nagaur, which at that time may have had some connections with the government of Sind or Multan. The tombs of Bhadreśvar are, therefore, amongst the earliest examples of a long tradition of the Indo-Muslims.

[76] K.A.C. Creswell, *The Muslim Architecture of Egypt*, II, Oxford, 1959, pl. 105a.

[77] S. Flury, *Ghazni, Le décor épigraphique des monuments de Ghazna*, Paris, 1925, pl. 6.

[78] *Ibid.*, 83-4, pls. 18 and 19.

[79] David Whitehouse, Excavations at Sīrāf, first interim report, *Iran*, VI, 1968, 20, pl. 8d; Second interim report, *Iran*, VII, 1969, 61-2; Fourth interim report, *Iran* IX, 1971, 16-17.

[80] Lucien Golvin, *Recherches archéologiques à la Qal'a des Banū Hammād*, Paris, 1965, 159, fig. 57.

[81] S. Zajadacz-Hastenrath, *Chaukhandigräber*, Wiesbaden, 1978, 99.

[82] M. Shokoohy, *Rajasthan*, I, Corpus Inscriptionum Iranicarum, Part IV, XLIX, London, 1986, pls. 70-1.

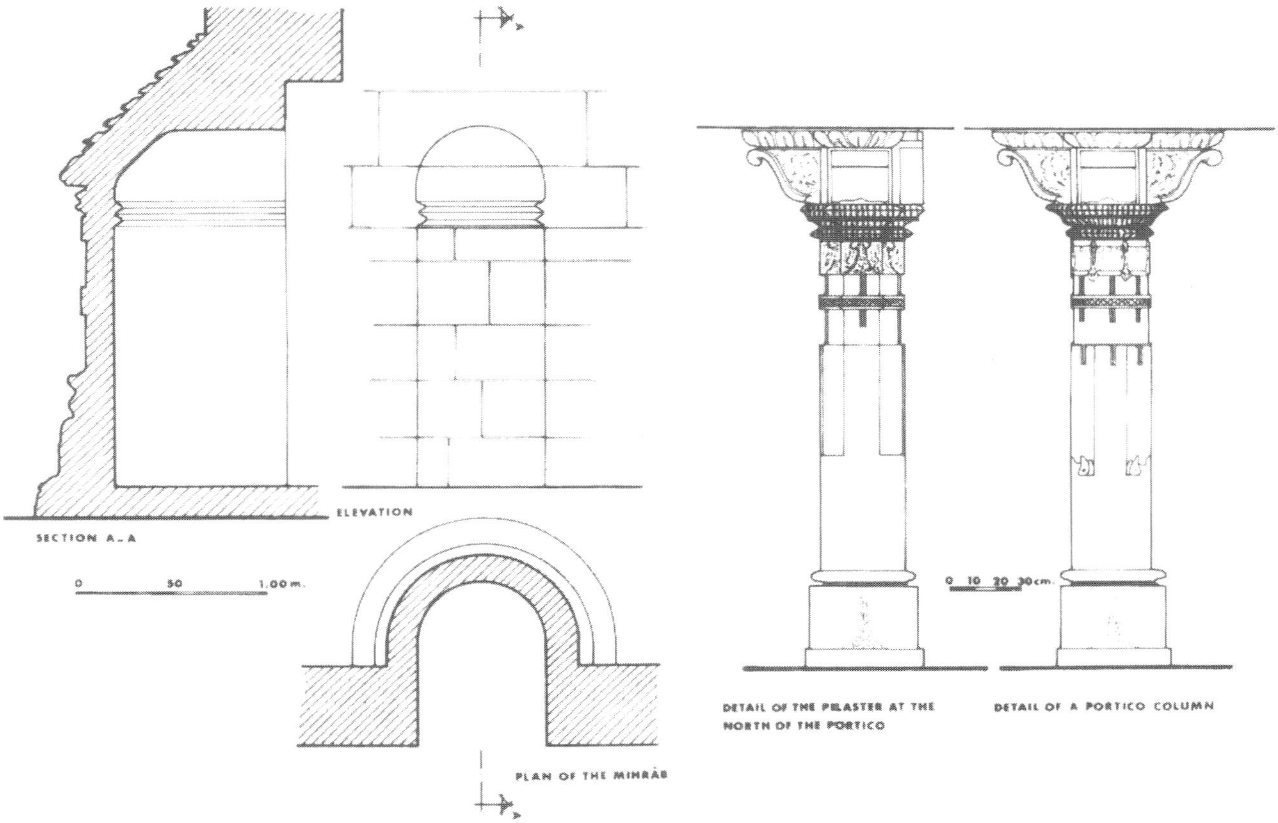

Fig. 9 The Shrine of Ibrāhīm, details of the *miḥrāb*, a pilaster and a column.

THE MOSQUES

Of the two mosques at Bhadreśvar, the larger stands about 150m. to the south-west of the temple compound and 110m. south-east of the Shrine of Ibrāhīm. It is called Solahkhambī by the local inhabitants and in our site plan the building is marked as Mosque 1 (fig. 2, pls. 1 and 12).

The Solahkhambī Masjid

The Solahkhambī Masjid (figs. 10-16, pls. 1, 12-21) stands at a lower level than the other buildings, and is now half buried in sand, and badly dilapidated. Many of its stones have been taken away, or scattered over the site. However, the remains of the building above ground level are sufficient to provide the basis for a ground plan. There was no attempt at excavation at the time of the survey, but surface sand was brushed away at the southern and western sides of the mosque, revealing that at least some of the buried parts of the building remain intact, and that only those elements protruding above ground seem to have been destroyed.

The plan of the mosque is of the Arab type, consisting of a colonnade around a central courtyard (fig. 10). The building is entirely constructed of large blocks of stone laid without mortar. Most of the columns and the lintels of the roof have survived, but only a few roof slabs still remained *in situ* (pl. 13). Nevertheless they provide enough evidence to show that the building had a flat roof. The roofed area on the *qibla* side was supported by two rows of columns, while the rest of the colonnade had only a single row (pl. 14a). An unusual feature of the mosque is an extremely wide portico at the eastern end of the building in front of the main entrance. This portico consists of four rows of eight columns each, making

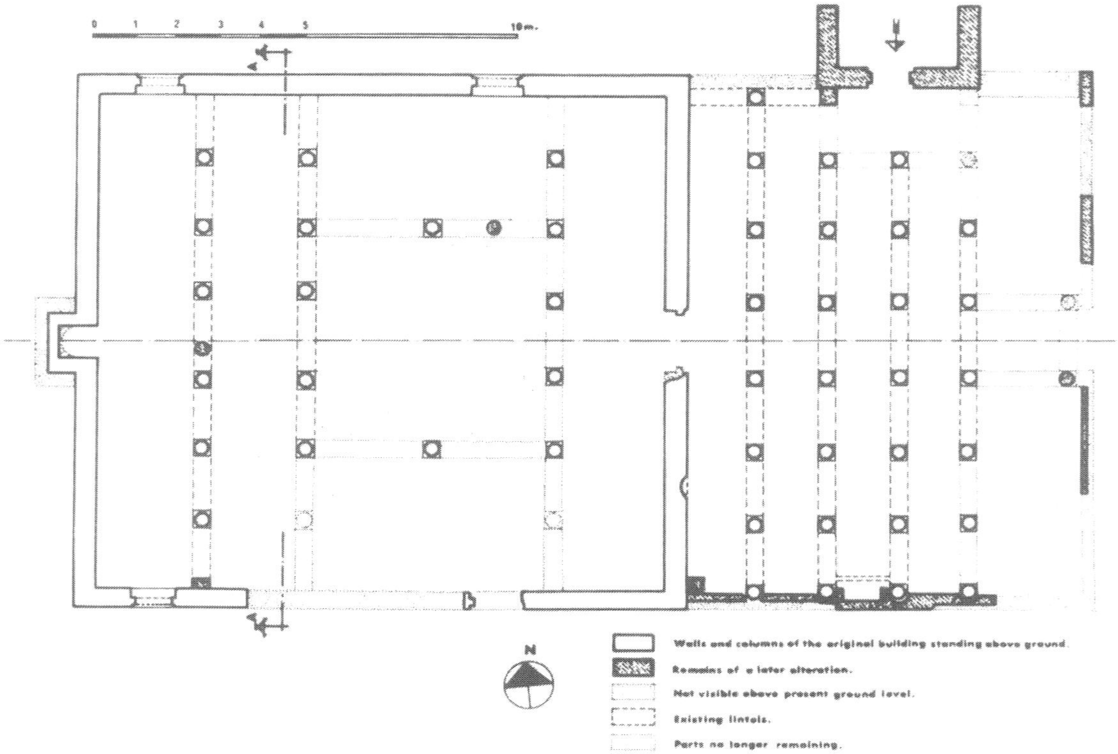

Fig. 10 Bhadreśvar, Solahkhambī Masjid, plan of the present structure.

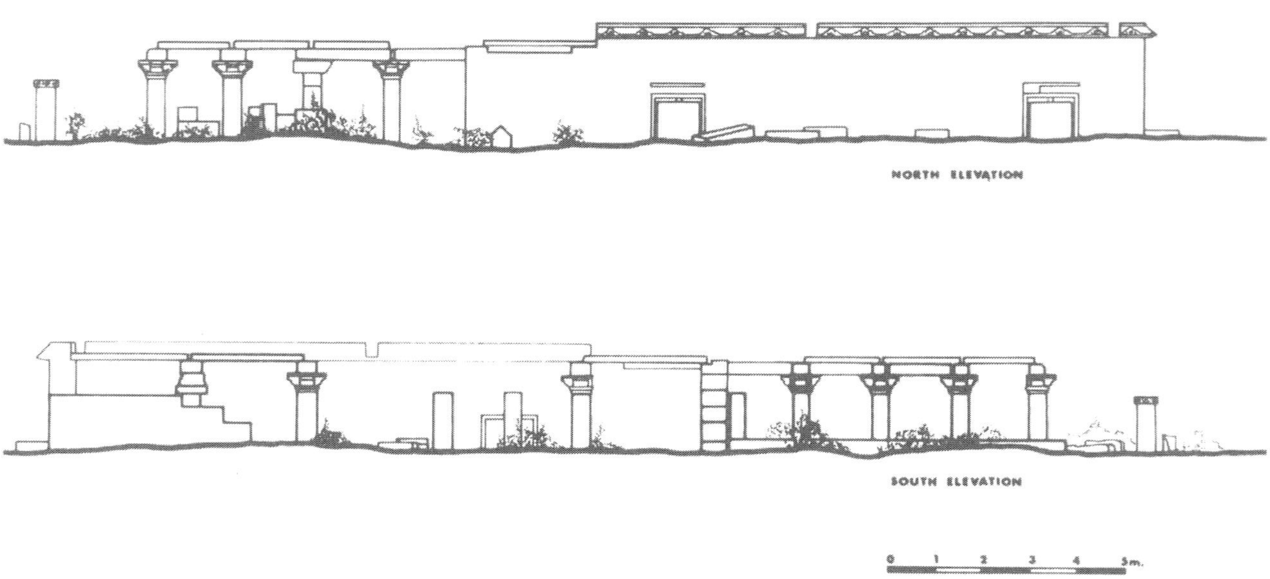

Fig. 11 Solahkhambī Masjid, north and south elevations.

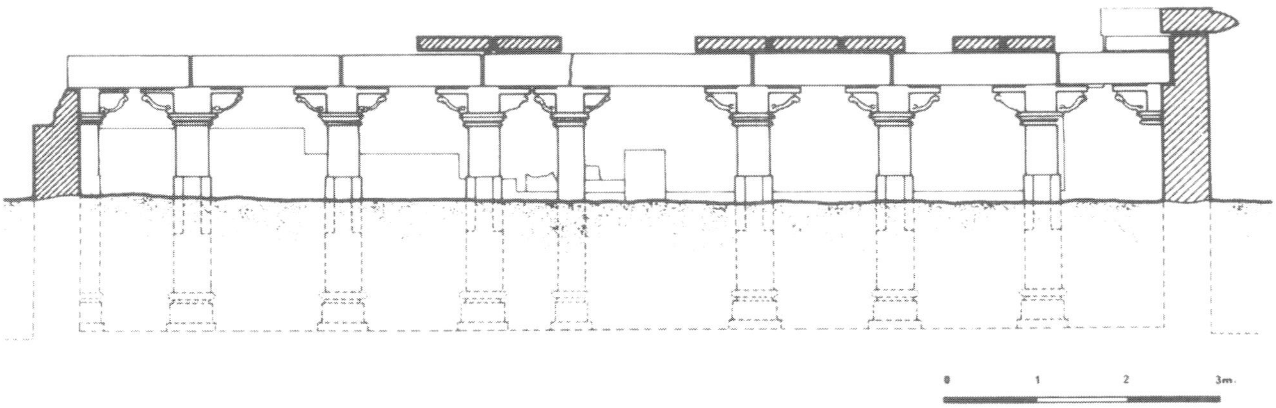

Fig. 12 Solahkhambī Masjid, section A-A through the prayer hall.

a total of thirty-two columns. The portico once provided a roofed space of 93 sq. m., which is not much less than the entire roofed space inside, originally about 130 sq. m. Such large porticoes are not a feature known in the mosques of that period elsewhere in the Islamic world, but may have been a local innovation, perhaps based on the Jain and Hindu open colonnades in Gujarat; for example that of the Jain temple at Pattadakal[83] and even those in very early Chalukyan monuments such as the temple of Meguti in Aihole.[84] The roof of the portico no longer exists, but many of the lintels and seven of the roof slabs still stand, showing that this section of the mosque also had a flat roof. On the ground lie flat slabs of stone, about 8 cm. thick, with mouldings on one side. Similar stones are used in the Shrine of Ibrāhīm as eave-stones to protect the portico against the rain (figs. 5, 7, pls. 2b, 4), and in the Solahkhambī Masjid eave-stones must have been provided all around the roof of the portico.

The lower parts of the columns, both in the portico and inside the mosque, are buried in the sand. However, the visible parts of their shafts, capitals and ante-capitals show that all the columns are made in the same form (fig. 13, pls. 17b, 18b, and 19). The monolithic shafts of the columns, like those of the Shrine of Ibrāhīm, are formed in three different registers — the lower part is square in plan, the middle octagonal, and the upper circular. Above each column was set a cushion shaped capital with a moulding underneath, and above that an ante-capital. The latter has the usual Indian-style brackets for supporting the lintels of the roof. The number of brackets varies from two to four, depending on the location of the column in question, and the number of lintels it supports. The ante-capitals of the north and south sides of the porch each have four brackets, since in addition to two side lintels and one cross lintel they also support the eave-stones along the cornice line. Those at the eastern end of the portico have three brackets, since they support the lintels of the colonnade on both sides, and also the eave-stones along the front end. The columns at the corner of the interior courtyard also support three brackets, as their position at the junction of the colonnades requires. In other positions, where only two lintels, one on either side, are needed, the ante-capitals have two brackets. In the Solahkhambī Masjid, in contrast with the Shrine of Ibrāhīm, the columns have little ornamentation, and the only decorations of the capitals and ante-capitals are simple mouldings. The lintels of the roof are also without adornment.

The mosque had originally only one entrance, in the middle of the east end under the portico. As far as its door frame is concerned, only a small part of the northern jamb (fig. 13, pl. 20a) is still visible *in situ*, as the depth of soil conceals the state of the threshold. The door lintel has also fallen, and is lying intact on the surface in front of the entrance (pl. 13b). These remains show that the entrance was decorated with lotus leaf foliation, of a pattern similar to that used at the entrance of the Shrine of Ibrāhīm.

The only wall of the mosque which still stands intact is that of the northern side (fig. 11, pls. 14b,

[83] Henry Cousens, *The Chalukyan Architecture*, ASI IS, XLII, 71, pls. 49b and 51.

[84] *Ibid.*, 29, pl. 4.

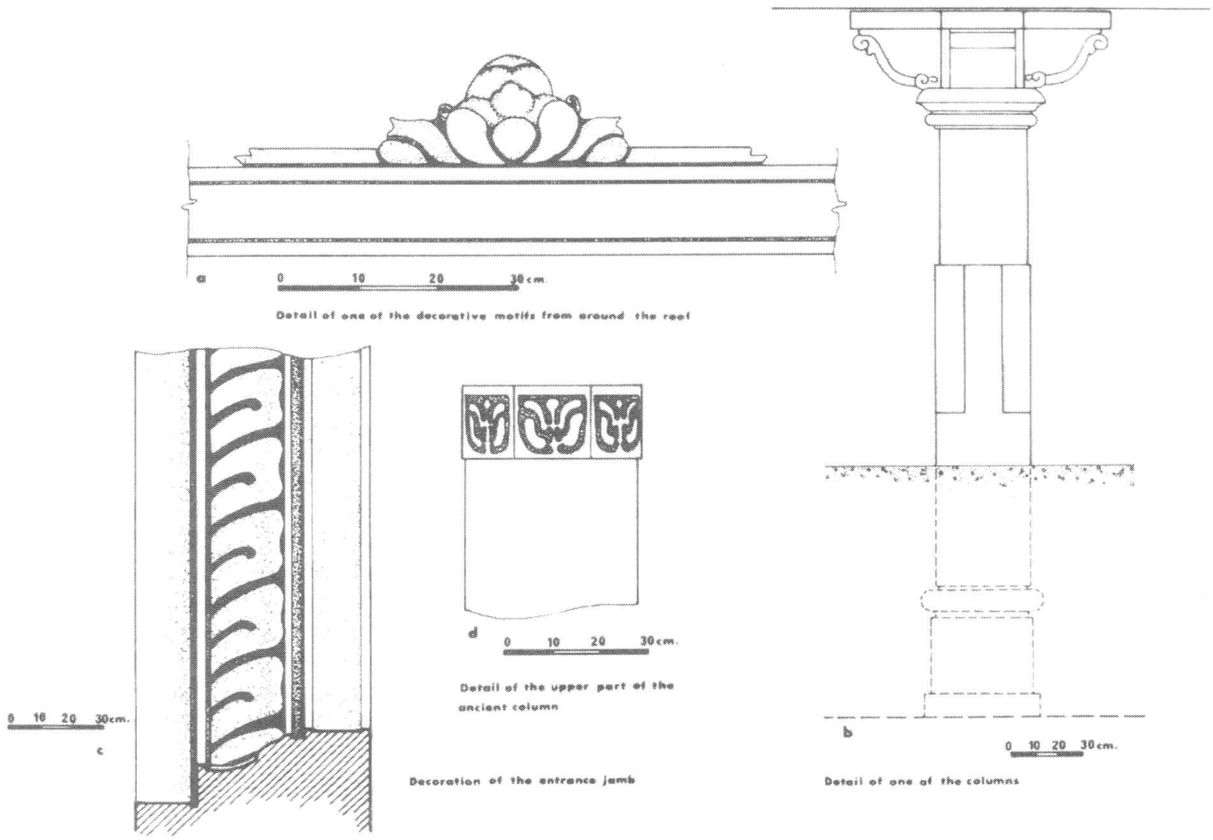

Fig. 13 Solahkhambī Masjid, details of the stonework.

15a). In this wall there are two windows, neither of which bears ornamentation. The remains of the southern wall are in ruins, but the portions above ground indicate that in this wall there were also two windows, opposite those of the northern wall (figs. 10 and 11). On the northern wall a few damaged sections of the eave-stones still remain in position, but naturally on the ruinous side of the southern wall they have entirely disappeared. Above the edge of the roof over the northern wall there are again a series of antefixae of the Indian form (pl. 15). They originally ran all round the roof, beneath the dripstones, but most of the latter have fallen, and several now lie on the ground nearby.

The *qibla* wall is also badly damaged, particularly in the middle section where the *miḥrāb* was located, as can be deduced from the recess visible in plan (figs. 10 and 14). In the photographs (pls. 16, 17a) vegetation conceals the profile of the lower courses of this *qibla* wall, but closer inspection of the *miḥrāb* shows it to be semi-circular in plan on the inside, though the projection on the outer face of the wall has square angles. It has been noted above that *miḥrābs* of this form are mostly seen in the early Umayyad period in Syria, and later in Sīrāf in the region of the Persian Gulf, as well as in the Fatimid epoch in northern Africa. The *miḥrāb* of the Solahkhambī masjid is especially similar to those of the Fatimid mosques of Madīnat al-Sulṭān[85] in Libya, and of al-Mahdīya[86] in Tunisia, as well as that of the Jāmi' of Dhū Jibla[87] in the Yemen, dated 481/1088-9.

[85] A. Abussaid, An early mosque at Medina Sultan, *Libya Antiqua*, III-IV, 1966-7, 155-60, fig. 1, pl. 47a.

[86] Alexandre Lézine, *Mahdiya, Recherches d'archéologie islamique*, Paris, 1965, 65, 74, pls. 30, 34.

[87] R. Lewcock and G.R. Smith, Two early mosques in the Yemen: a preliminary report, *Art and Archaeology Research Papers*, IV, 1973, 121, pl. 123, fig. 5.

In the Solahkhambī Masjid there is also a secondary *miḥrāb* located within the portico, that is to say, outside the eastern wall of the mosque enclosure and on the south side of the entrance (pls. 17b and 18a). This *miḥrāb* has survived in better condition than the other, and its upper portion is also preserved. It has the form of a shallow recess, segmental in plan, but it does not project on the other side of the wall which forms part of the interior facade of the mosque. Above this *miḥrāb*, like that of the Shrine of Ibrāhīm, there is a slab carved in the form of a semi-circular arch, and once more, around the springing of the arch there are two projecting mouldings. As already suggested, these mouldings may have functioned as slots into which a decorated medium of hard material, probably wood, could have been fitted. The destroyed portion of the main *miḥrāb* of the mosque would have had the same structural form as the subsidiary *miḥrāb*, since as we shall see all the *miḥrābs* of Bhadreśvar are of a similar shape.

In the portico of the Solahkhambī Masjid traces of some later building work can also be seen. At the northern side three of the original columns have been removed and replaced by an entrance (fig. 10, pl. 21a). Remains of a secondary wall can also be seen all around the portico. Most of the stones reused in this wall were originally taken from the roof slabs. Even the eave-stones of the portico have been reused in this secondary wall (pl. 20b). In the south side of the portico an altar has been set up (pl. 21c), suggesting that in the course of secondary use this area of the mosque was used as a temple. Even more curious is a feature occurring at the eastern end of the portico, 1.6m. from the first row of columns. Here stands another column of a totally different form, about which it could be suggested that it may have been employed from an unknown building of earlier date. The intrusive column is a monolithic cylinder, with a band of floral decoration at the top of the shaft (fig. 13, pl. 21b). The pattern of this ornamentation resembles the anthemion ornamentation on many of the Aśokan columns, for example, those on the elephant capital at Sankīsā,[88] on the lion column at Sānchī,[89] and on the bull capital at Rāmpūrva.[90] It has already been noted that during the late 2nd century A.D. at the time of Ptolemy, Bhadreśvar was an important city and the capital of a local kingdom. This unusual column, with its reminiscence of Aśokan architecture, indicates that an ancient Indian monument belonging to an earlier style than the mediaeval monuments of Bhadreśvar once existed in the neighbourhood. What that earlier style may have been is not easy to infer, but in view of the important role played, possibly by the Indo-Greeks and certainly by the western Satraps — whose activity in the region is attested by the monuments at Girnār and who survived until the 4th century A.D. — we may consider that our column preserves an echo of the successors of Aśoka in the region. More probably, the style represented might be that of the Western Satraps. We can assume that this column must have been re-erected in the mosque at the time of its conversion to a temple.

Returning now to the description of the mosque, in spite of the present dilapidation of the building and the disturbance of the original plan of its portico, the surviving remains provide all the information required to produce conjectural reconstruction drawings of the original building. The conjecturally reconstructed plan and two elevations given in this report (figs. 14 to 16) are based on this evidence. They show a substantial and impressive building. It need hardly be said that if it were at any time possible to clear the accumulated sand, and by excavation to expose the original floor levels, and at the same time to re-erect the scattered stones, a large number of which seem to be present on the site, an imposing monument could be seen in all its magnificence. At the same time the clearance of the surrounding ground level would show what earlier buildings had stood in the vicinity, and would throw light on the mysterious "intrusive column" reused in the secondary stage of the construction of the portico. Little or nothing is at present known of the pre-Gupta culture of this area, so that both operations are likely to be rewarding from the scientific point of view, and also to encourage interested visitors to come to the site.

Outside the mosque lie three tombstones, one to the north and two to the north-west. They all consist of the usual horizontal slabs with gabled top, similar to those in the courtyard of the Shrine of Ibrāhīm. Each of the tombs bears a dated inscription, those to the north-west reading 573/1177[91] (pl. 46), and 624/

[88] John Irwin, Aśokan pillars: a reassessment of the evidence - II, structure, *The Burlington Magazine*, CXVI, 1974, 717, fig. 6.

[89] John Irwin, Aśokan pillars: a reassessment of the evidence, *The Burlington Magazine*, CXV, 1973, 709, fig. 6.

[90] *Ibid.*, 709, fig. 7.

[91] Z.A. Desai, Kufic epitaphs from Bhadreśwar in Gujarat, *Epigraphia Indica, Arabic and Persian Supplement*, 6, inscription 6; M. Bayani-Wolpert, no. 3 of the present report, Part 2.

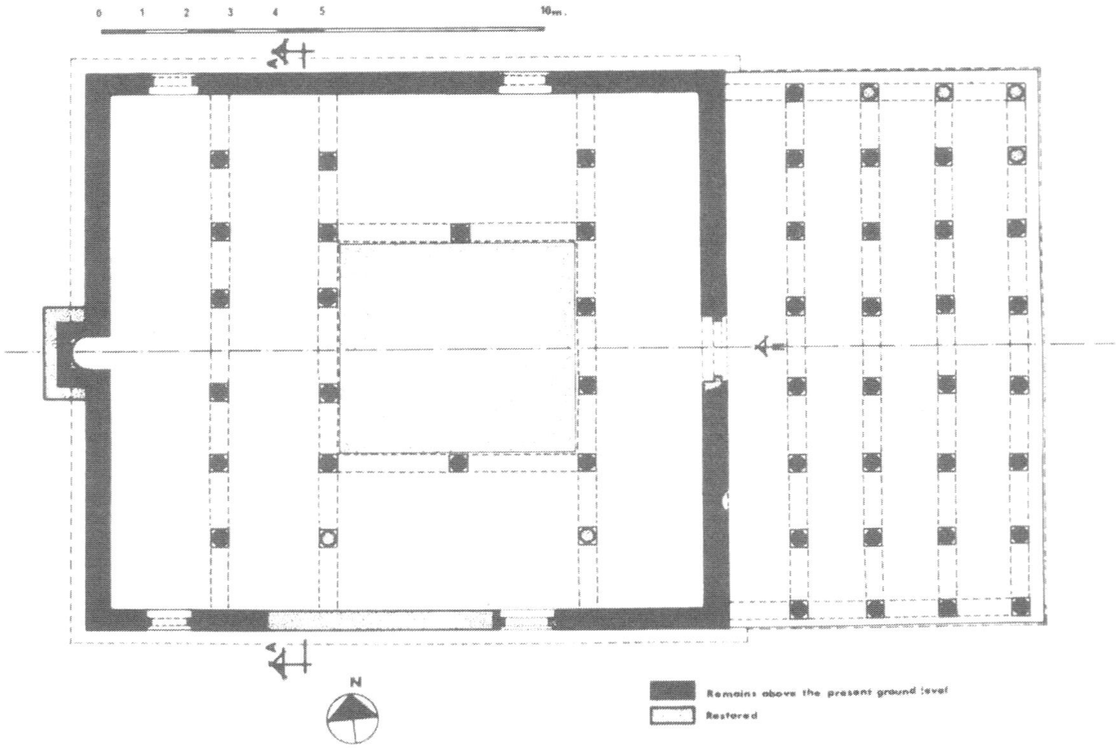

Fig. 14 Solahkhambī Masjid, plan, conjectural restoration.

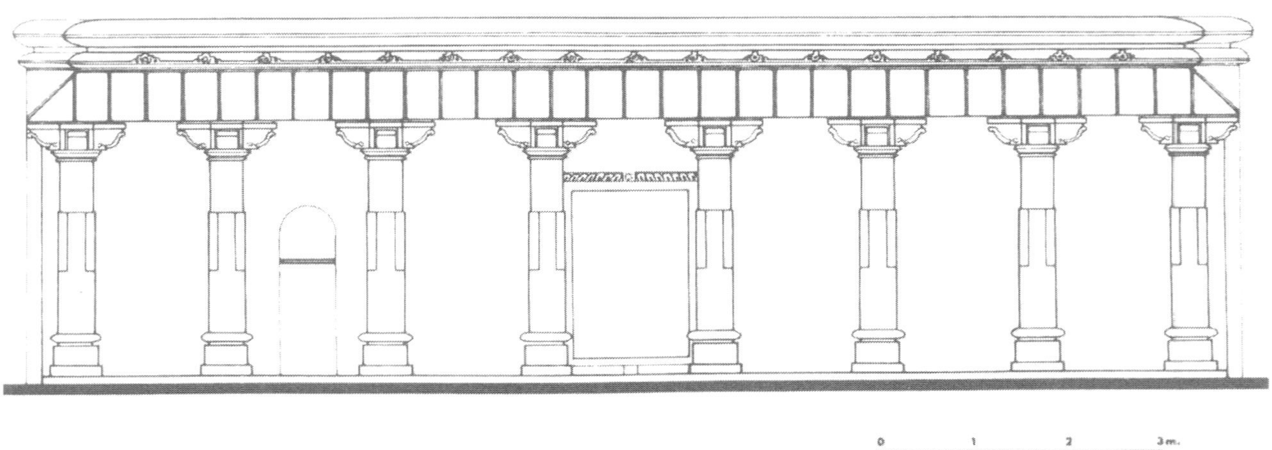

Fig. 15 Solahkhambī Masjid, east elevation, conjectural restoration.

1227[92] (pl. 47a), and that to the north 62[?]/1224-31[93] (pl. 47b). These tombs will naturally belong to the time when the mosque was in regular use. Therefore the time of the construction of the Solahkhambī Masjid

[92] Desai, *op. cit.*, 7, inscription 7; Bayani-Wolpert, no. 4 of the present report.

[93] Desai, *op. cit.*, 8, inscription 8; Bayani-Wolpert, no. 5 of the present report.

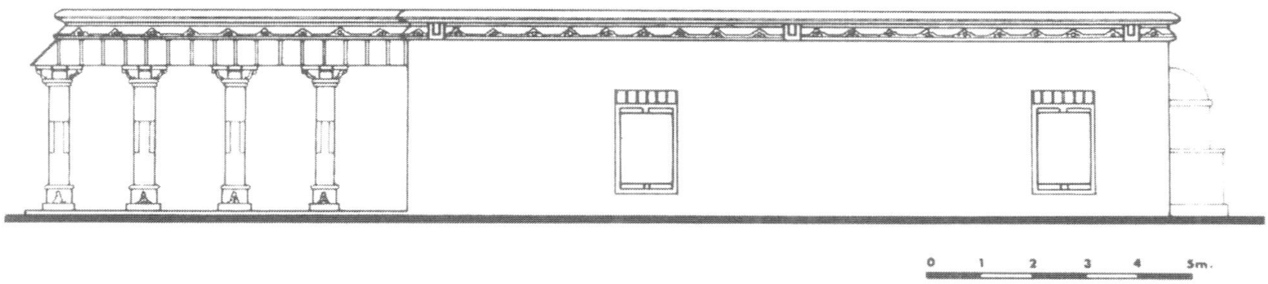

Fig. 16 Solahkhambī Masjid, north elevation, conjectural restoration.

goes back at least as far as 573/1177-8. We have already seen that the Jain chronicle and the *Jagadu-charita* speak of the building of a mosque for the local Muslims at the time of the restoration of the town and its temple in V.E. 1223/A.D. 1166. This date is only eleven years earlier than the date of the oldest tombstone. On the other hand it must be noted that of the two mosques of Bhadreśvar, the Solahkhambī Masjid is much the larger, and indeed must have been the main congregational mosque (the *jāmi' masjid*) of the city. The date mentioned in the chronicle may, therefore, be accepted for the beginning of the construction of this mosque. In this case the Solahkhambī Masjid would have been built only six years later than the Shrine of Ibrāhīm. This mosque is important not only for its size and elaborate structure, but also as representing the earliest standing mosque of India, and one the historical origins of which raise many unusual questions.

The Chhoṭī Masjid

The second mosque of Bhadreśvar, referred to in this report as the Chhoṭī Masjid (the small mosque), and marked in the plan as Mosque 2, is located about 140m. north-west of the Solahkhambī Masjid and about 50m. south-west of the Shrine of Ibrāhīm (fig. 2). The Chhoṭī Masjid (figs. 17-28, pls. 1, 22-33) stands on a platform 45cm. higher than the present ground level. The platform measures 15.20 × 20.50m. and its exterior revetment is faced with large blocks of stone, while the core is filled with stone rubble. The mosque itself is entirely built of large stone blocks similar to those of the shrine and the Solahkhambī Masjid. The plan of the mosque consists of a courtyard, with a double colonnade at the *qibla* end, and a sanctuary chamber containing the principal *miḥrāb* (fig. 17). Of the original courtyard at present little can be seen, since a secondary chamber occupies most of its area. Moreover the north-eastern and south-eastern corners of the original courtyard have been demolished and their stones reused in this chamber. However, most of the remainder of the walls and the three original entrances to the courtyard have survived (figs. 18, 19, 26, pls. 22, 23a). This slight damage to the layout therefore offers little hindrance to the preparation of a conjecturally reconstructed plan (fig. 28).

Of the three entrances mentioned, the main one is that at the eastern end (fig. 26, pl. 23a). The frame of the doorway is decorated with garland patterns and "diamonds and discs" framed by lotus leaf foliation. This decoration closely resembles that of the Shrine of Ibrāhīm. It may be suggested, therefore, that they both belong to the same period, and were the work of the same team. Although this doorway survives intact, it no longer affords access to the building, on account of the later constructions in the courtyard.

The two other entrances to the courtyard are located on the northern and southern walls, opposite each other. That on the south is now blocked with stone rubble, but the northern entrance is still in use. Both of these entrances are decorated in the same style as the eastern entrance.

The colonnade of the mosque stands along the western side of the courtyard (fig. 21, pls. 24, 25). It has a flat roof supported by two rows of columns. Each row contains four free-standing columns and two engaged columns on the inner face of the projecting walls. Like those of the Shrine of Ibrāhīm, both the free-standing and the engaged columns are monolithic, but stand on separate square bases. They have the usual cushion shaped capitals and ante-capitals (pl. 28a). Their shafts, again like those of the other monuments, are formed in registers — square, octagonal, and circular (fig. 25). The necks of the shafts are decorated with "pot and foliage" motifs, strings

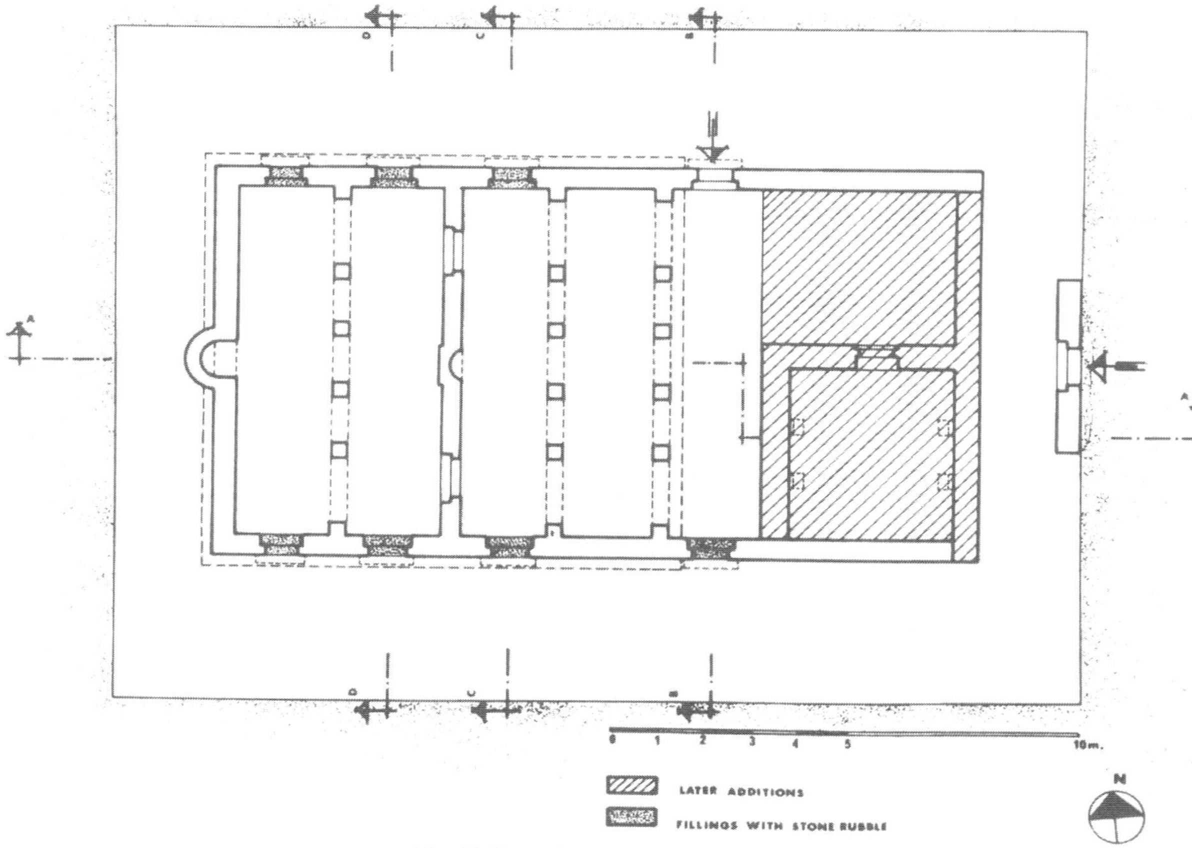

Fig. 17 Bhadreśvar, Chhoṭī Masjid, plan.

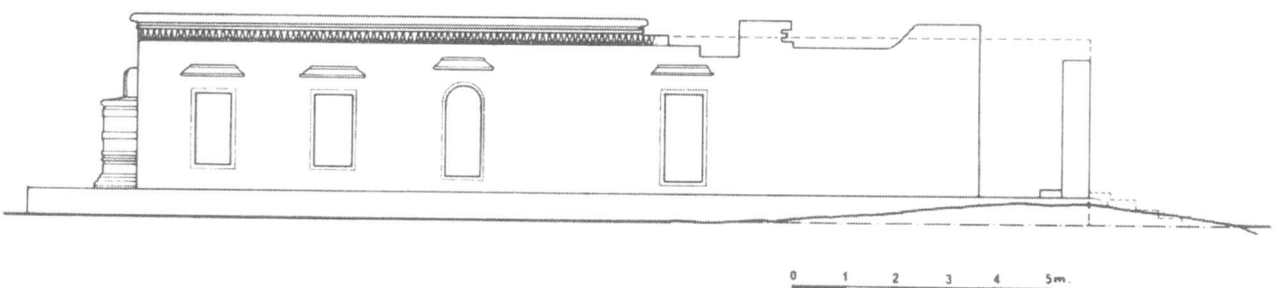

Fig. 18 Chhoṭī Masjid, south elevation.

of beads, and "diamond and disc" collars. This decoration is also very close to that of the Shrine of Ibrāhīm. Even the technique of carving and the precise details of the motifs are similar in these two buildings. This close analogy is another indication that the Chhoṭī Masjid must have been built at the same period as the shrine.

In the colonnade of the Chhoṭī Masjid the lintels supporting the roof slabs are also decorated (fig. 25, pl. 24). The faces of the lintels are each divided into two horizontal registers — the upper bears a decoration of diamond motifs, while the lower is ornamented with garlands similar to those on the entrances. The underside of each lintel is decorated with a lotus

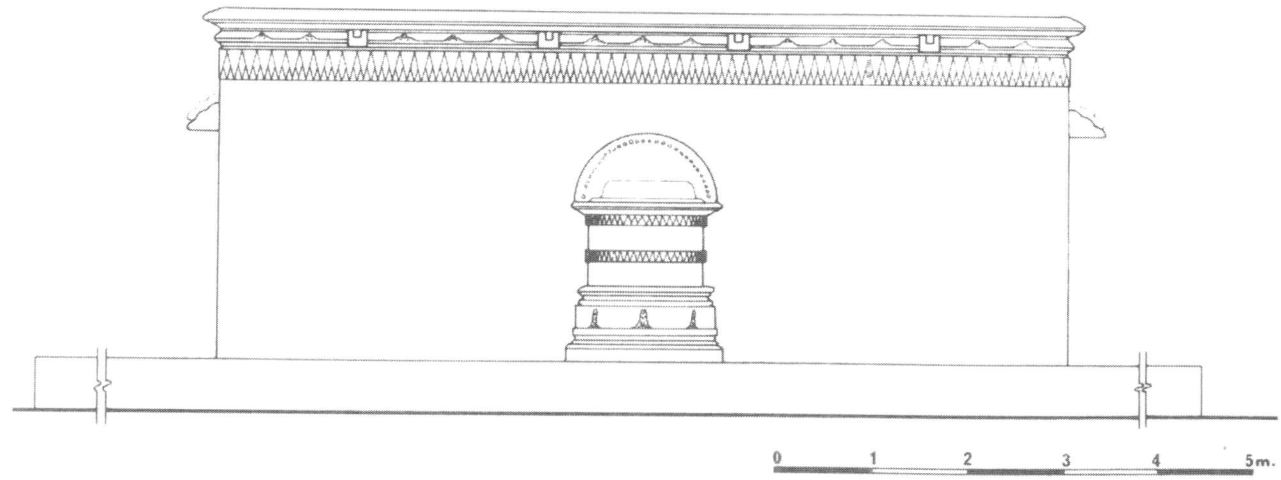

Fig. 19 Chhoṭī Masjid, west elevation.

Fig. 20 Chhoṭī Masjid, section A-A through the mosque and the later structure in the courtyard.

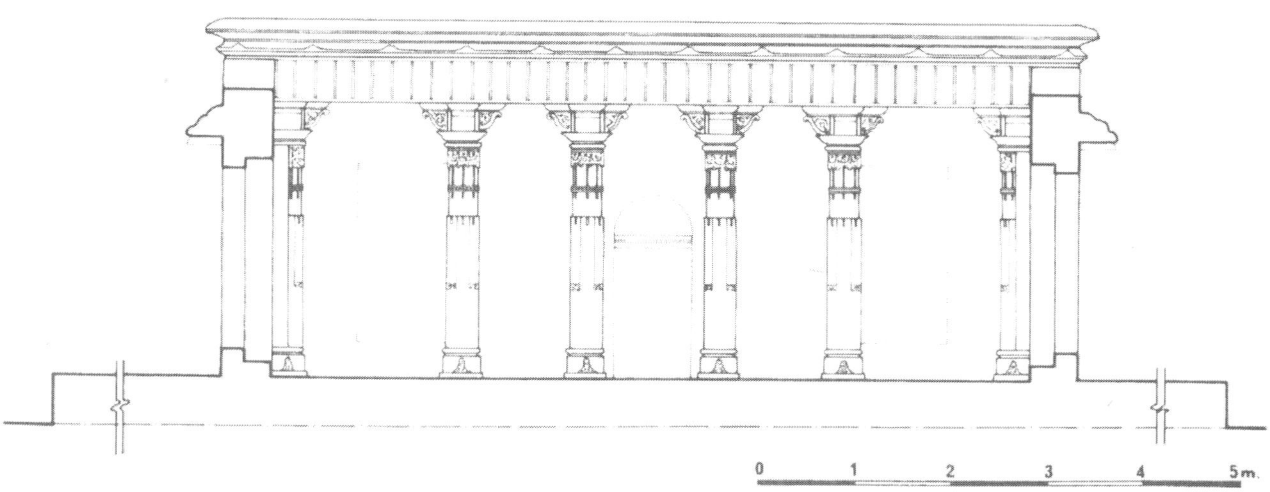

Fig. 21 Chhoṭī Masjid, section B-B through the courtyard, showing the façade of the colonnade.

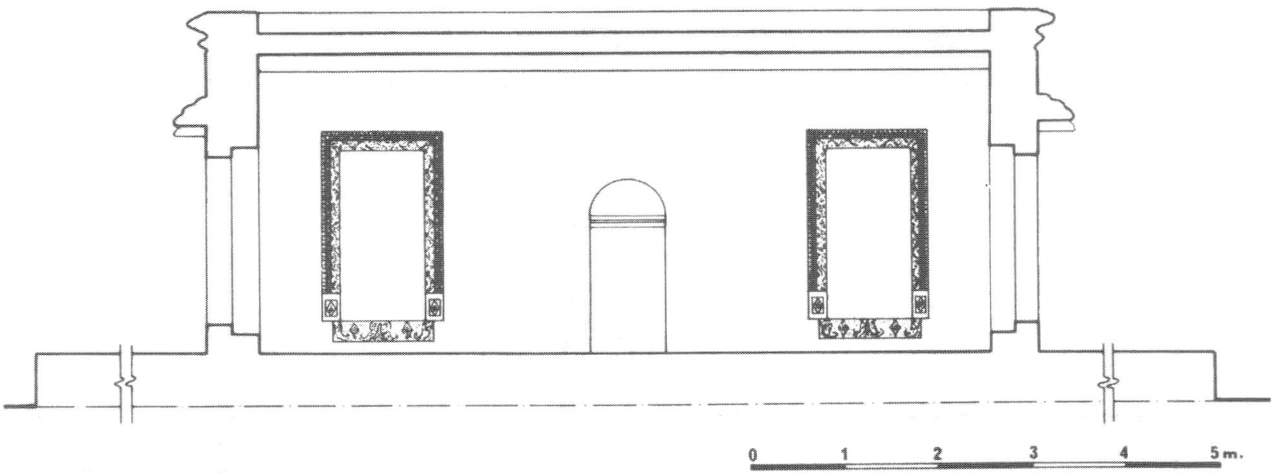

Fig. 22 Chhoṭī Masjid, section C-C through the colonnade, showing its western wall with the subsidiary *miḥrāb* and the entrances to the sanctuary.

Fig. 23 Chhoṭī Masjid, section D-D through the sanctuary.

rosette in a manner similar to those of the Shrine of Ibrāhīm.

At the front of the colonnade and above the first row of columns, eave-stones were originally provided, of which some still stand *in situ* (pl. 25a). Since parts of some of the stones have fallen, the section through some of the eave-stones has become visible, together with that of the entablature. The eave-stones are supported by stub-lintels standing on the front bracket of the ante-capitals (fig. 24). The upper sides of these stub-lintels are sloped to provide the angle for the eave. This setting does not of itself prevent the eave-stones from slipping down. That function is performed by a projecting tab on the eave-stones, which rests on top of the main lintel, and is held down by the weight of the massive drip-stones standing partly upon the eaves, and partly on the roof-slabs. The eaves are therefore supported by a kind of cantilever effect. However, this kind of structure does not possess any great stability. Even where the drip-stones have remained in place, some of the eaves have already fallen, presumably because the tolerance of the slot was too great. Thus even small movements in the foundations allowed them to work loose. Of course,

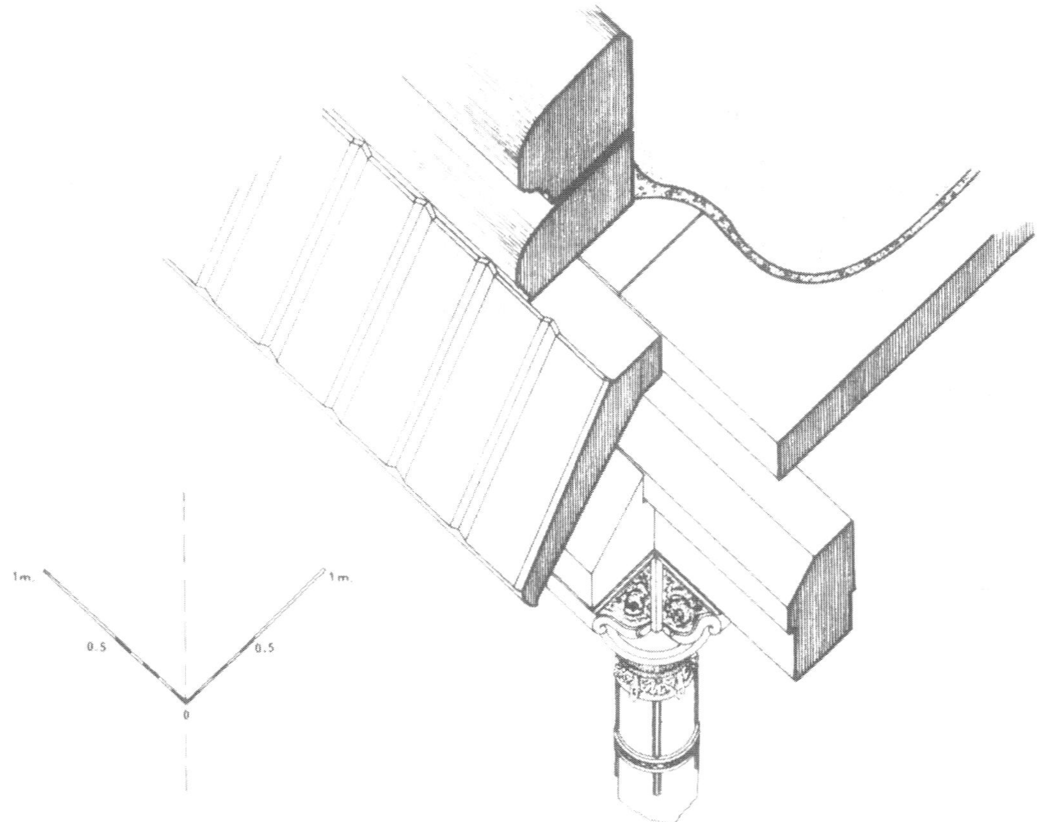

Fig. 24 Chhoṭī Masjid, perspective drawing of the roof structure.

where the drip-stones were removed or fell, the eaves would collapse immediately. Some of the eaves have already fallen, and the others are in imminent danger of collapse. In the case of the Solahkhambī Masjid we have already seen that none of its eave-stones, constructed in a similar way, has remained *in situ*.

The colonnade of the Chhoṭī Masjid has two doorways opening directly to the outside, apart from the access through the courtyard. These doorways are opposite each other, but are now blocked with stone rubble. Both doorways have the usual decorations. Their interesting feature is, however, the upper lintel, which is hollowed on the inside in the form of a semi-circular arch (fig. 27, pl. 26a). We have already seen that the *miḥrābs* of the other monuments at Bhadreśvar have lintels carved in the form of semi-circular arches, but in this mosque the arch form appears on the facade and above a doorway. As noted, the semi-circular arch is not a feature of Indian architecture. Neither does this arch profile appear in the later Islamic buildings of India influenced by the Iranian and Central Asian style. By the time the arch makes its appearance, the pointed forms were everywhere present. However, in the 12th century semi-circular arches were still common in Syria and North Africa. The appearance of semi-circular arches on Mosque 2 is therefore another indication of an Arab link with the Muslim community of Bhadreśvar.

In the colonnade of the Chhoṭī Masjid there is a *miḥrāb* situated in the centre of its *qibla* wall (fig. 22, pl. 26b). The *miḥrāb* is of the familiar type, already seen in the previous monuments — semi-circular in plan, and with a lintel carved in the form of a semi-circular arch above. Like the other *miḥrābs*, this one is also plain, but has the usual projecting mouldings around the springing of its arch. This *miḥrāb*, however, projects only minimally beyond its wall, which separates the colonnade from the sanctuary chamber. At either side of the *miḥrāb* are doorways opening into this chamber (fig. 22, pl. 27). The frames of both are

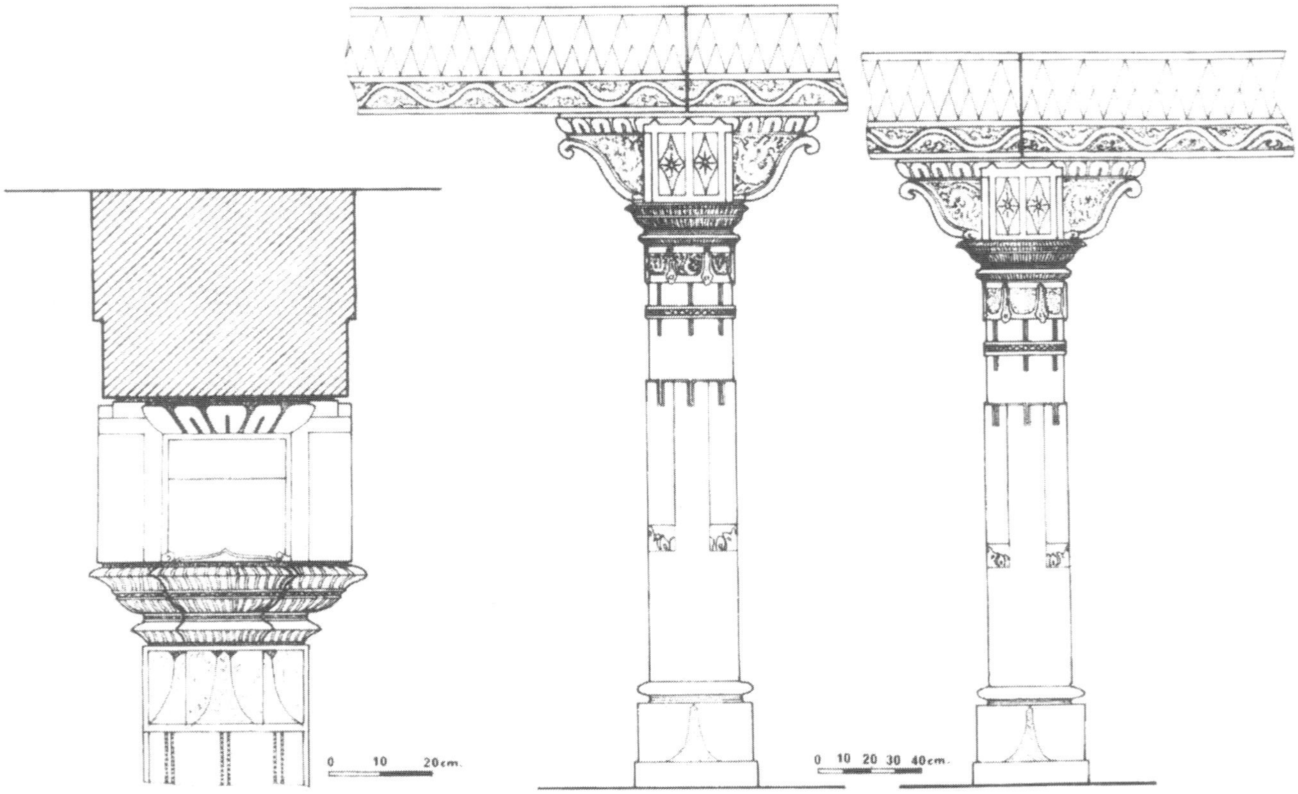

Fig. 25 Chhoṭī Masjid, details of the stonework of the columns and the lintels.

decorated in a manner similar to the other entrances. However, these decorations are on the outer side, the inside of the doorway being entirely plain.

The sanctuary chamber of the mosque (figs. 20 and 23, pls. 28b, 29, and 30a) measures 4.24 × 7.83m. from wall to wall, and so approximates to a double square. Its floor rises 40cm. higher than that of the colonnade, but the flat roofs are at the same level. Thus the interior height of 3.00m. in the chamber is 40cm. less than that of the portico. Across the chamber there is a row of columns, four free-standing and two engaged. These columns have once more the usual capitals and ante-capitals, and support the roof slabs by means of stone lintels. All the components of the columns, together with the ante-capitals and the lintels, are decorated in the same style as those of the colonnade (pls. 30, 31). The chamber has four windows, two in the northern and two in the southern wall (pl. 29b). The windows again have decorations similar to those of the doorways. All of these windows are now blocked with stone. On the *qibla* wall of the chamber is a *miḥrāb* larger than that of the portico. It is a slightly stilted semi-circle in plan, 81cm. wide, and in depth as much as 90cm. As to elevation the general form is again similar to the other *miḥrābs* in Bhadreśvar, having the familiar semi-circular arch and projecting mouldings at the level of the springing. In this *miḥrāb* alone, however, the ceiling is not hemispherical, but is backed with a flat block of stone, providing above the springing only a flattened recess (pls. 28b, 32a).

The *miḥrāb* projects beyond the outer line of its wall as in the Shrine of Ibrāhīm (fig. 19, pls. 23b, 32b). However, unlike the latter, the roof of the projection is not conical, but is covered by the same single block of stone as is seen on the inside, which on the exterior is carved to a semi-circular outline.

Except on the eastern front of the colonnade, eave stones are not provided at the Chhoṭī Masjid. Instead, every door and window has its own eaves. Along the

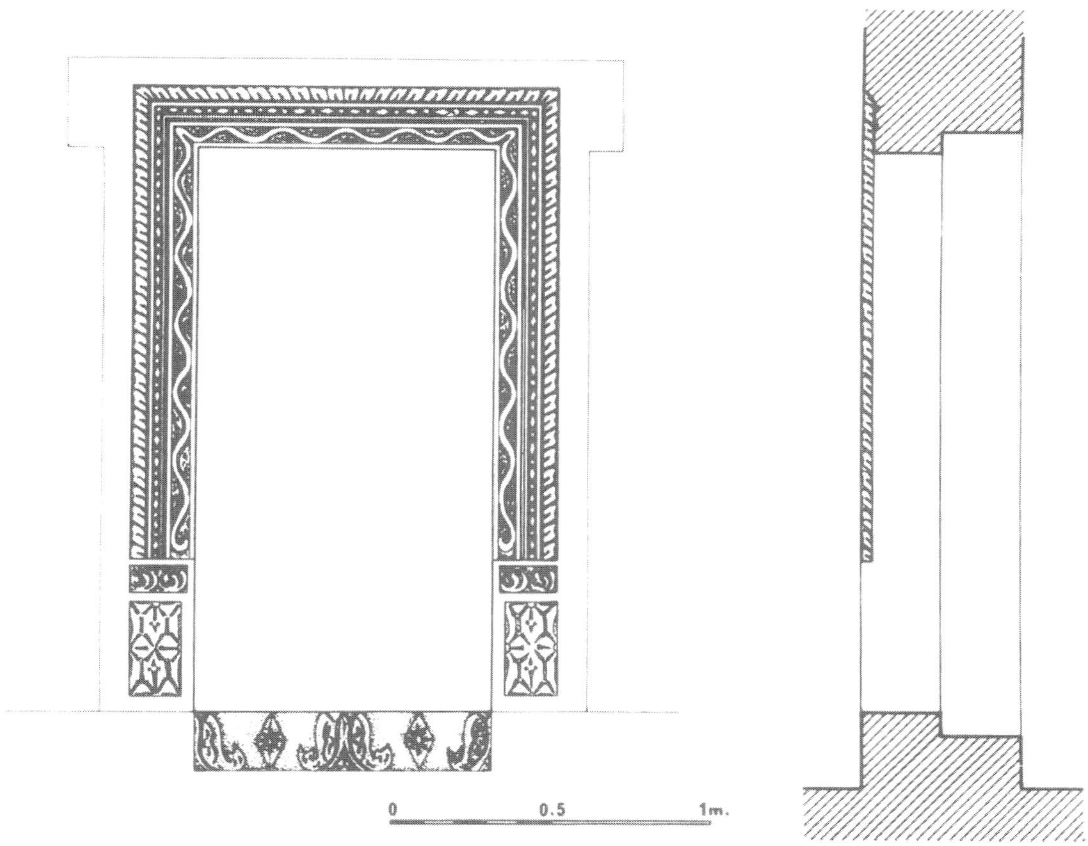

Fig. 26 Chhoṭī Masjid, detail of the eastern entrance to the courtyard.

exterior faces, all around the roof, drip stones are set as a cornice (figs. 18 and 19, pls. 22, 23b). The lower part of this cornice is once again decorated with antefixae similar to those of the Solahkhambī Masjid; and below it runs a frieze decorated with diamond patterns, a familiar form already seen in the Shrine of Ibrāhīm. The rainwater is carried clear of the building by means of four water spouts, all located at the western side of the building (fig. 19, pls. 23b, 32b). The water spouts are also made of stone.

The building has now been abandoned, but the later constructions on the site indicate that it was reused at a later date. With the exception of the northern entrance to the courtyard, all other doorways and windows have been blocked, and parts of the walls of the courtyard have been removed. Inside the courtyard, and only 2.2m. from the colonnade to the east, a platform 85cm. high has been raised. On the southern side of this platform a square chamber has been built (fig. 17 and 20, pl. 33). This chamber was left unfinished and without a roof. However, remains of the footings of two transverse arches inside the chamber show that it must have been planned to have a vaulted roof. The chamber has a north-south orientation, similar to that of the main Jain temple of Bhadreśvar, and the later structure of the portico of the Solahkhambī Masjid. It may be suggested therefore, that the later alterations of the Chhoṭī Masjid were also devised for the purpose of providing a temple, which remained unfinished.

As far as the dating of the original mosque is concerned, there is no inscription on the stone-work, nor are there any tombs nearby. For this reason dating is only possible by a comparison of the structure with the other monuments of Bhadreśvar. We have already seen that not only the style of construction of the Chhoṭī Masjid but also the decoration is similar to that of the other monuments. In fact the

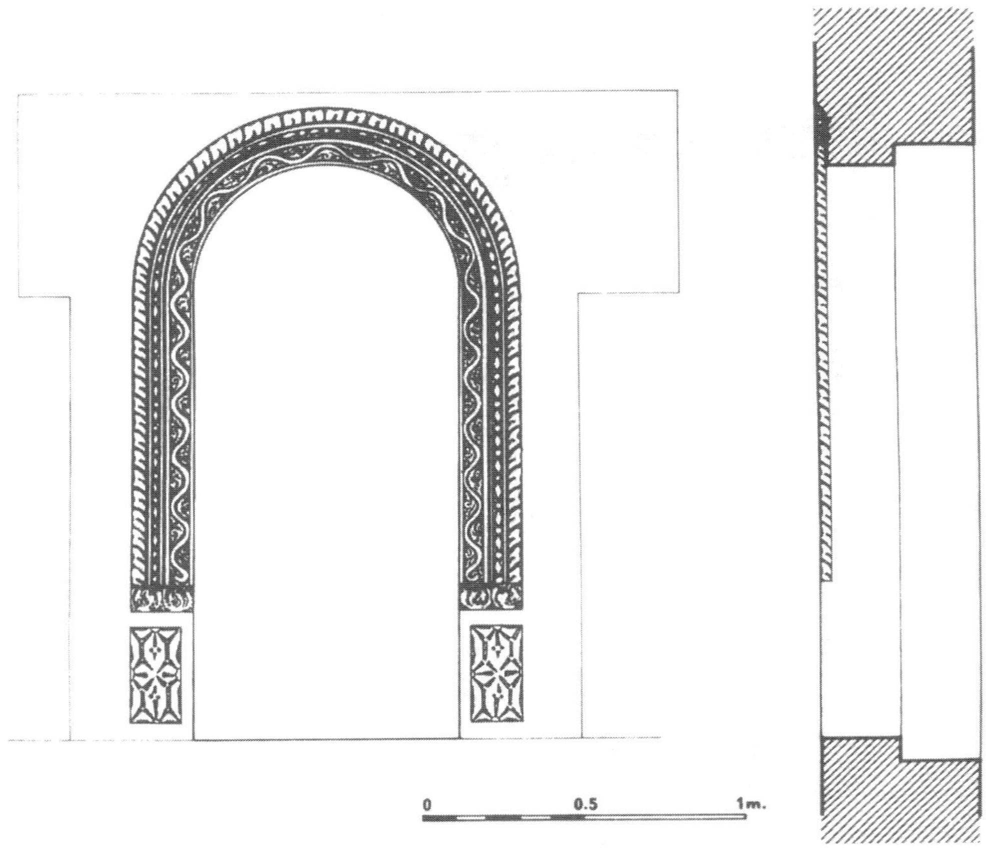

Fig. 27 Chhoṭī Masjid, detail of the northern arched entrance to the colonnade.

Chhoṭī Masjid and the Shrine of Ibrāhīm are so close in this respect that they must have been executed by the same team of workmen. The Chhoṭī Masjid therefore could have been built at the same time as the Shrine of Ibrāhīm, and consequently not much later than A.D. 1160.

OTHER ARCHITECTURAL REMAINS

Two other ancient structures of Bhadreśvar are located to the east of the Jain temple (fig. 2). They are a square pavilion known locally as the Chatri (the common term for an open domed structure standing on columns), and a well-reservoir known as the Dūdhā Wāv.

The Chatri

The Chatri (figs. 29-32, pls. 1, and 34-7) is situated to the east of the temple and 45m. east of the ruins of the ancient wall. In Burgess's report[94] he speaks of a structure which he calls the "Dūdhā Temple", and assumes to be Jain, but which the present writer was unable to identify. He then speaks of the Chatri as a ruined shrine of this "Dūdhā Temple", but close examination of the construction proved that it is an individual structure and not an extension of another building, of whatever period. In the present writer's opinion, Burgess's reference to the "Dūdhā Temple" arises from a misconception derived from the manuscript, and in fact no traces of a structure which could be described by this name can be seen on the ground.

[94] *Report on the Antiquities of Kaṭhiawād and Kachh*, 1874-5, ASWI, II, 1876, 206.

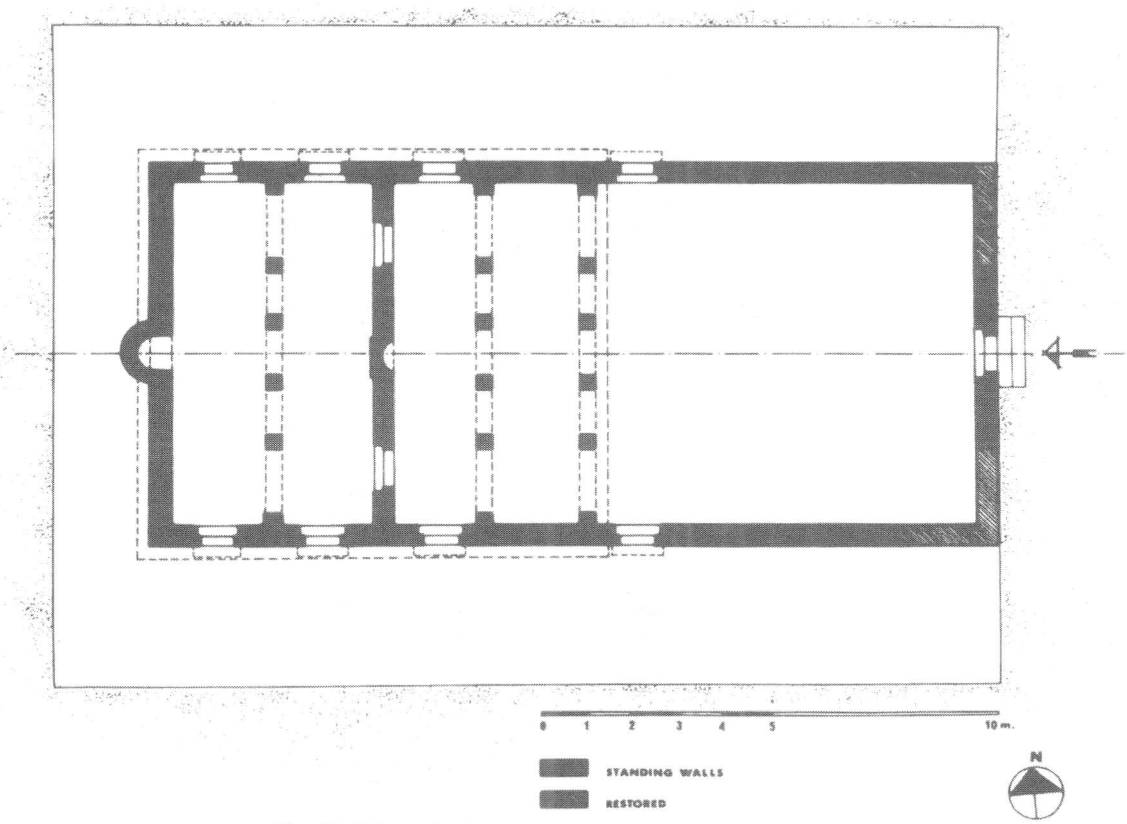

Fig. 28 Chhoṭī Masjid, plan of the mosque in its original state.

The Chatri consists of twelve columns supporting a corbelled dome, all still in a fair state of preservation (figs. 30 and 31, pls. 34-6). It stands above a single pyramidal, but originally stepped, platform built with large stone blocks. Most of the stone steps, however, have now been removed, and the remainder are buried under earth and bushes. Only the upper side of the platform, measuring 4.98m. square, still remains intact. The columns (fig. 32, pl. 35) have monolithic shafts, and are carved in the same style as those of the other monuments. They stand on the usual square bases decorated with a floral triangular motif (fig. 32, pl. 37b). Similar decoration can be seen on the bases of the columns of both the Shrine of Ibrāhīm and of the Chhoṭī Masjid. Above these bases the monolithic columns have once more three registers: square underneath, octagonal in the middle, and circular at the top. Above the shafts are first the usual cushion-shaped capitals and then ante-capitals (pl. 36a). The shafts bear no decoration, and the capitals and ante-capitals are decorated with simple mouldings. These columns closely resemble those of the Solahkhambī Masjid, not only in their shape and decoration, but also in size and proportions. It must be noted that the Jain columns of Bhadreśvar, already illustrated in the Burgess report,[95] differ totally from these columns. They are much taller than those of the Islamic buildings, and have only two main registers, as well as being decorated in a different manner. Therefore it is more likely that the Chatri was associated originally with the Muslim community of Bhadreśvar, in which case the name used by Burgess, "Dūdhā Temple", would not be appropriate for this monument.

The Chatri is roofed with a corbelled dome, supported by means of stone lintels standing on the ante-capitals (pl. 36). The outer edges of the upper sides of the lintels are bevelled. This feature has already

[95] *Ibid.*, pl. 40.

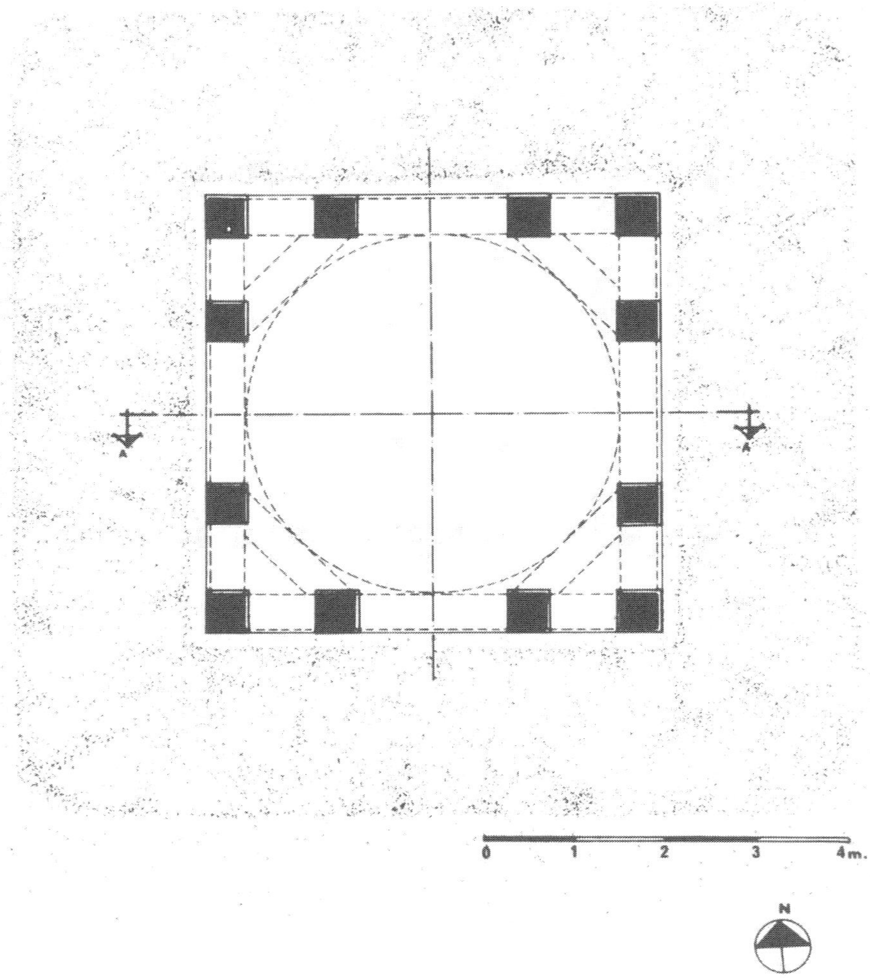

Fig. 29 Bhadreśvar, the Chatri, plan.

been noticed in the lintels of the Islamic buildings of Bhadreśvar, and indicates that eave-stones must have been set above the lintels (fig. 31). However, the eave-stones themselves no longer survive.

The dome is constructed of large stone blocks smoothed only on the inside (pl. 36), but with a rough surface on the outer sides (pl. 34). The use of this method of stone-dressing shows that the exterior of the dome would have been finished with a covering (fig. 31). In most cases cement mortar was used for this purpose. This technique was very common in Rajasthan and Gujarat during the 13th century, and most well known monuments, for example the mosque of Aṛhāī din kā Jhoṅpṛā in Ajmer,[96] have the same type of dome. It must be noted that the soft and light cement used for the finishing of such domes was particularly suitable for an Islamic building, since it helped to give the dome a hemispherical outline. To achieve such a shape by the dressing of the stones alone is rather impractical for a corbelled dome, as it introduces a disproportionately heavy load. The intended domed form of the Chatri may therefore be another indication of Islamic origin for the monument.

The stone-work of the dome is decorated on the inside only with simple mouldings. Between the ends of the lintels, however, there are decorative stub lintels,

[96] James Fergusson, *History of Indian and Eastern Architecture*, revised edition, II, London, 1910, 230.

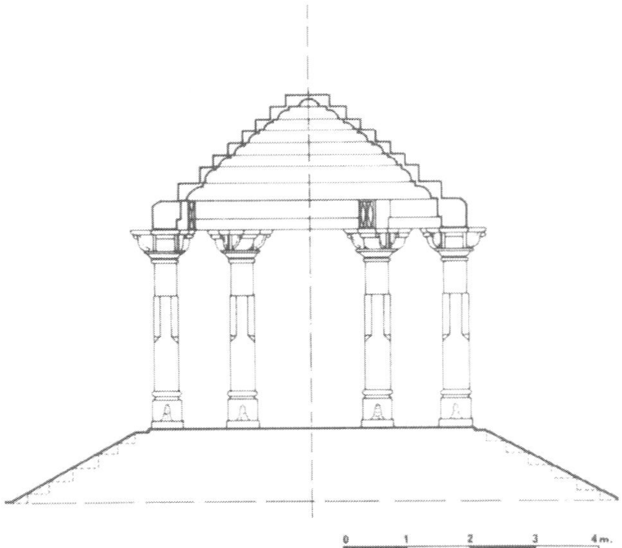

Fig. 30 The Chatri, section A-A.

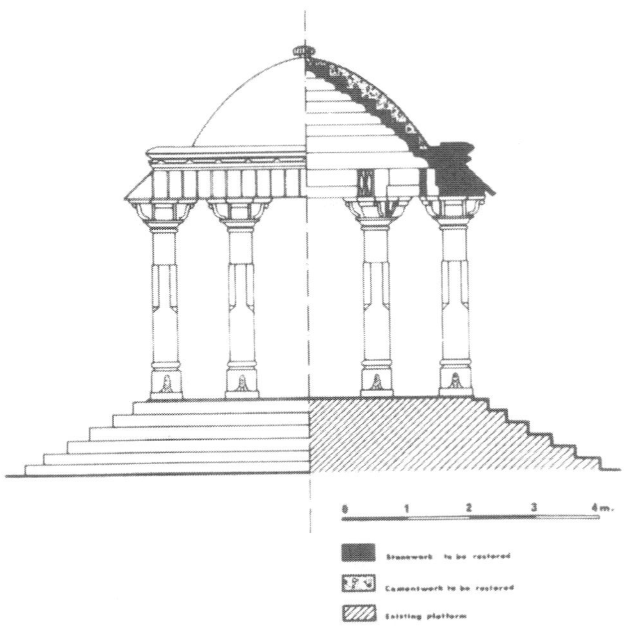

Fig. 31 The Chatri, north elevation and section A-A, conjectural restoration.

four surviving *in situ*, of which the inside faces are enriched with diamond motifs of two distinct varieties (fig. 32, pl. 37a). There are similar motifs at the Shrine of Ibrāhīm and at the Chhoṭī Masjid, where, however, the designs are more elaborate.

As far as the function of the building is concerned we have already noted that, in spite of Burgess's suggestion, the building is not part of a larger temple, but was originally designed as an individual chatri. Its Jain origin is also not certain, since both the design of its columns and its dome suggest an Islamic origin. During the Islamic period in India single chatris were widely used for tomb structures, and many such buildings can be seen among the monuments of the Delhi Sultanate.[97] The tradition survived for a long period, and its characteristics are well preserved in a series of later (17th century) examples at Thatha in Sind.[98] It is therefore permissible to conclude that the chatri at Bhadreśvar was a Muslim tomb, and this building may then represent the earliest recorded example of the type.

The Dūdhā Wāv

The well-reservoir complex (figs. 33-5, pls. 38-42) known as the Dūdhā Wāv is located 50m. north of the Chatri. It is built entirely of large stone blocks set in layers in the usual manner, without mortar. The structure is now in a ruinous condition, with its lower parts buried in sediment, and many of the upper stones removed (figs. 34, 35). Although it still contains water, it is no longer in use. The complex consists of a large well at the eastern, and a long narrow tank at the western, end. These two portions are connected by means of an aperture in their dividing wall four metres below ground level (pl. 41b). Waterworks of this kind are common in both Hindu and Muslim settlements in Gujarat, as well as elsewhere in western India. The best examples of the type are the Bai Ḥarīr Wāv[99] in Ahmadabad, and the well-reservoirs at Adalaj,[100] Isanpur,[101] and Asarwa.[102] The Dūdhā Wāv is, however, less grandiose than the works mentioned. Its plan more closely resembles the

[97] Friedrich Wetzel, *Islamische Grabbauten in Indien*, Leipzig, 1918, reprinted, Osnabrück, 1970, 13-25; Tatsuro Yamamoto, *Delhi*, I, Tokyo, 1967, 85-9, pls. 109-118, Tombs nos. 101-129.

[98] Henry Cousens, *The Antiquities of Sindh with Historical Outline*, ASI, XLVI, Imperial Series, Calcutta, 1929, 115-18, pls. 35, 55, and 56.

[99] James Burgess, *The Muhammadan Architecture of Ahmadabad*, ii, ASWI, VIII, London, 1905, 4-6, pls. 3, 15 and 16.

[100] *Ibid.*, 10-13, pls. 6 and 12.

[101] *Ibid.*, 13, pl. 23.

[102] *Ibid.*, 1-3, pls. 2 and 13.

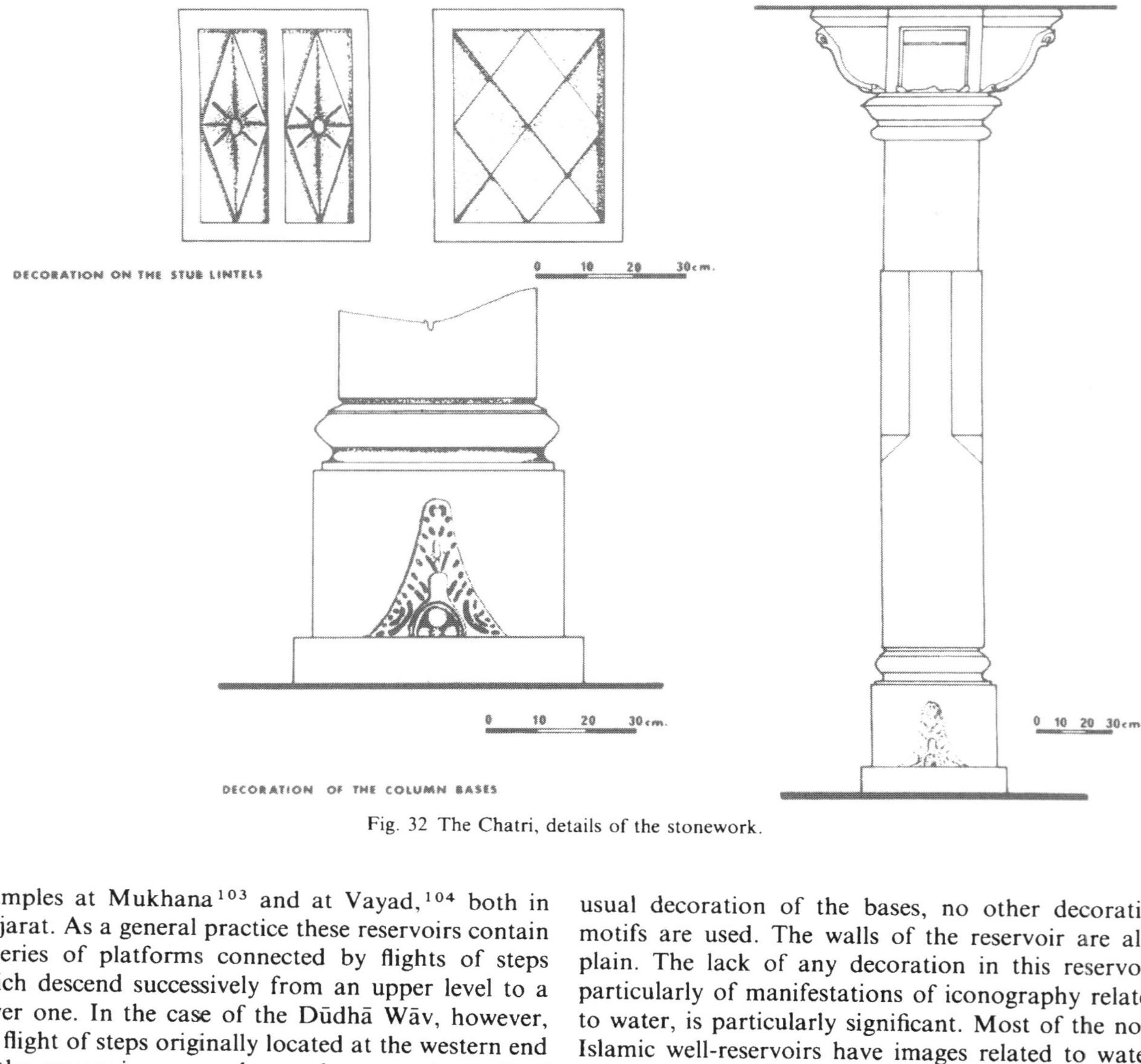

Fig. 32 The Chatri, details of the stonework.

examples at Mukhana[103] and at Vayad,[104] both in Gujarat. As a general practice these reservoirs contain a series of platforms connected by flights of steps which descend successively from an upper level to a lower one. In the case of the Dūdhā Wāv, however, the flight of steps originally located at the western end of the reservoir can no longer be seen, since all of its stonework has been removed. Nevertheless the sloping foundation of the stairs still survives (pl. 39a). Three of the platforms remain, each standing on four columns. The superstructure of the western and central platforms has now disappeared, but the western one preserves its columns and the lintels of its roof (fig. 35, pls. 39b, 40b). The columns of the reservoir once more have the familiar shape, a shaft with three registers: square, octagonal, and circular. These columns are similar to those of the Solahkhambī Masjid and of the Chatri, both in their general form and in their details. Apart from the simple mouldings and the usual decoration of the bases, no other decorative motifs are used. The walls of the reservoir are also plain. The lack of any decoration in this reservoir, particularly of manifestations of iconography related to water, is particularly significant. Most of the non-Islamic well-reservoirs have images related to water. In the case of some works, for example the Adalaj Wāv, Hindu images are used even under Muslim patronage. At the Dūdhā Wāv, therefore, the absence of icons shows that even if the complex was not entirely built for the members of the Muslim community, we may suppose that regard for their wealth and

[103] J. Burgess, *Report on the Antiquities of Kaṭhiawād and Kachh*, ASWI, II, London, 1876, pl. 69.

[104] J. Burgess and H. Cousens, *The Architectural Antiquities of Northern Gujarat*, ASWI, IX, Calcutta, 1903, 112-13, pls. 54-6.

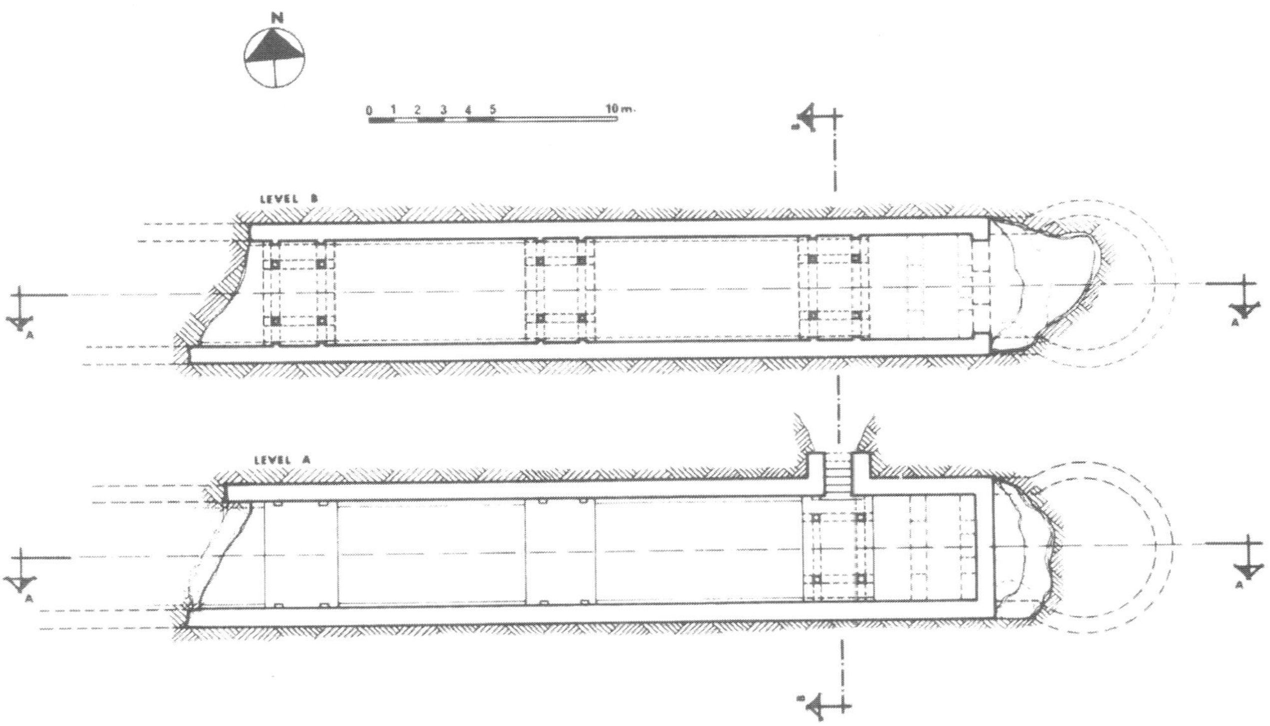

Fig. 33 Bhadreśvar, the Dūdhā Wāv, plan.

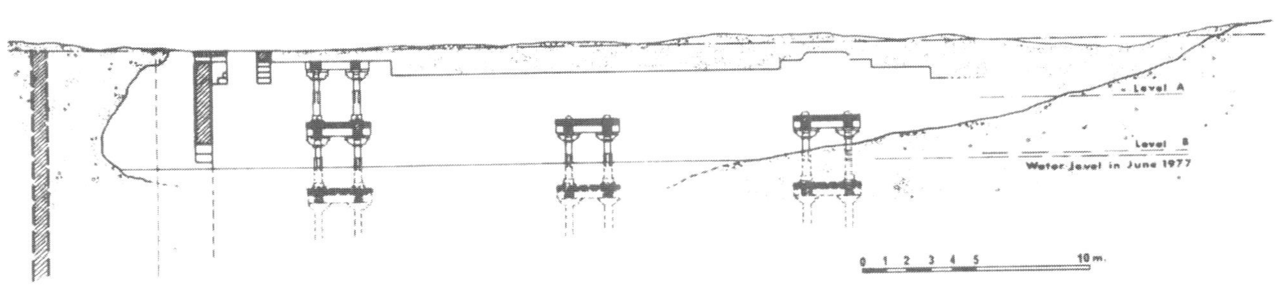

Fig. 34 The Dūdhā Wāv, section A-A.

influence caused the builders to pay special attention to their preferences.

In the Dūdhā Wāv little can be seen of the well at the eastern end, since most of the stones of its wall have been removed, and the shaft is filled with earth to within 7m. of ground level. The top of the well is now covered partly by secondary brickwork, and partly by mud and rubble (pl. 42b). However, a small hole has been opened at the south-western corner, giving access to the well.

Next to the wall and around the top of the reservoir there are six corbels built out from the reservoir walls (pl. 41). Four are on the eastern end, and the other two face each other on the northern and southern sides respectively. Each of these corbels consists of four superimposed cantilever stones, of which the upper ones are larger than the lower. On the two northern and southern corbels lies a massive stone lintel 63 × 56cm. thick and 4.38m. long. This lintel must have been intended to carry a heavy load. The

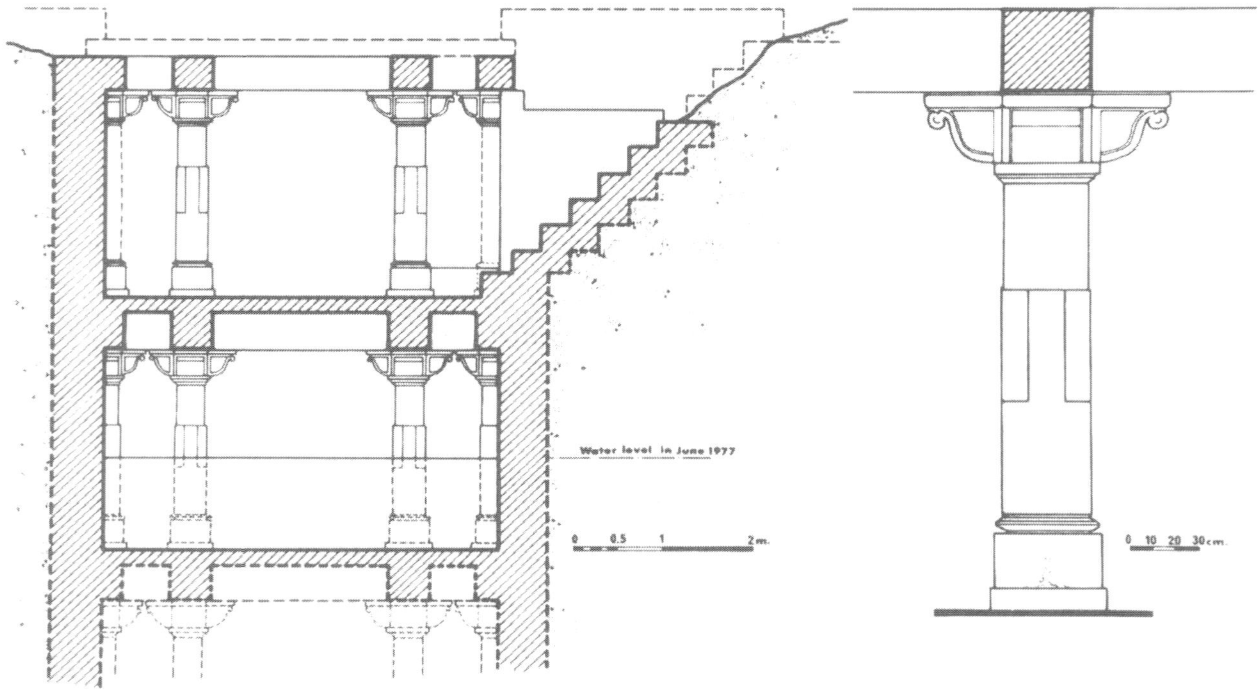

Fig. 35 The Dūdhā Wāv, section B-B, and detail of a column.

arrangement of the corbels and lintel suggests that they were intended to support a structure, probably a chatri. Indeed most of these well installations, for example Bai Ḥarīr in Ahmadabad and Jethabhai Mulji at Isanpur, still preserve a chatri. The reservoir at Vayad, which as we have already noted has a plan similar to that of the Dūdhā Wāv, retains a chatri above the reservoir, adjacent to the wall. It stands in the same position as the structure assumed for the Dūdhā Wāv. At Vayad the chatri is relatively small and has only four columns, two standing on the stone lintel, and the other two on the corbels which project from the eastern wall.

For a possible indication of the dating of the Dūdhā Wāv, the *Jagaducharita*[105] mentions that at the time of the reconstruction of Bhadreśvar, besides the restoration of the temple and the building of the mosque, a *wāv* was also constructed. The similarity of both the style of construction and the shape of the columns at the Dūdhā Wāv and the Solahkhambī Masjid likewise suggests that they could have been built simultaneously. In that case the Dūdhā Wāv would have been constructed around 1175, which is also close to the suggested date for the Solahkhambī Masjid.

CONCLUSION

The site of Bhadreśvar in the north-east corner of the Gulf of Kachh has a Jain temple, reported by Burgess in 1875, together with some early Islamic monuments. In 1965 Dr. Z.A. Desai published the Arabic inscriptions associated with the latter buildings. The date of the earliest, 554/1159-60, establishes it as the earliest recorded Muslim structure of India,[106] built almost half a century prior to the establishment of the Delhi Sultanate. The Muslim buildings are thus of considerable interest, while the site in addition claims a long history going back to the *Mahābhārata*, and is probably Ptolomy's Bardaxema (a fortified city on the

[105] G. Bühler, *The Jagaducharita of Sarvanada*, Wien, 1892, 7.

[106] The only other building in the subcontinent considered by some scholars to date from the mid-12th century and prior to the establishment of the sultanate of Delhi is the tomb of Shāh Yūsuf Gardīzī in Multan, Pakistan. While the cubical form of the building

"Kanti Gulf"), and al-Bīrūnī's Bhadra (located with Kachh east of Daybul and towards Somnath). The earliest Muslim raid on the area was that of Maḥmūd of Ghazna, who captured Bhīswāra (416/1025-6), but, according to the *Bantvijaya Chronicle*, after the departure of the Muslims the local Jain ruler re-established control over the city. This chronicle and the *Jagaducharita* both mention a Jain ruler and merchant, Jagadeva, whose dates embrace those of the Islamic monuments. The latter chronicle even mentions a mosque built at this time for the Ismā'īlī community of the city. Manijeh Bayani-Wolpert shows us that the character of the floriated Kufic inscriptions is indeed typical of the Fatimid work of North Africa, and that the inscriptions emphasise the special position of these Ismā'īlī settlements, which were protected by the local Indian rulers, to whom the settlers were felt to present no threat because they also resisted the advancing sultanate forces.

Now the site stands over one kilometre north of the shoreline. The outline of the fortification can no longer be traced, but a section of ruined wall, 120m. in length and built of large blocks of stone still stands above ground on the eastern side of the site. This wall may have been part of the ancient circumvallation. The present village occupies part of the western side of the site, and many of its buildings are constructed of reused stones from older structures. About 200m. further to the east stands the great Jain temple, which, together with its many modern buildings, is surrounded by an enclosure wall. Outside the enclosure and to the north is an old well, the circular shaft of which is lined with blocks of stone. There is a niche lined with similar stones below ground level on the eastern side of the shaft. This niche could have been used as a vantage point by those drawing water from the well. However, while it still contains water, the well is no longer in use.

The Islamic monuments are located on the southwestern side of the site, between the village and the temple. They consist of two mosques, the larger one known locally as the Solahkhambī, and a shrine with an inscription in which the name Ibrāhīm is mentioned, but which is locally attributed to Shaikh 'Uthmān Marwandī, known as Makhdūm La'l Shahbāz, who actually died at Sehwan in 673/1274-5, and whose tomb there is still regarded as a holy shrine. Thus while Burgess and Desai both refer to the structure as that of La'l Shahbāz, in this report it is designated the Shrine of Ibrāhīm. This is the dated structure bearing the inscription of 554/1159-60. There are also two other ancient constructions at the east of the site, a domed pavilion known as the Chatri, and a well-reservoir known as the Dūdhā Wāv.

These structures share the same method of construction and the same forms of stone carving and decoration. They are all built of large blocks of stone, evenly cut and laid without mortar, a technique well known in India, particularly in Gujarat, since ancient times. The roofs are supported by stone lintels surmounting columns and pilasters. The Indian style columns are all monolithic, with square, octagonal, and circular registers. This is the characteristic local form for the shaft of a *linga*. Though Indian Muslims would not have been unaware of the significance of this form, nevertheless the community at Bhadreśvar appear to have regarded it with tolerance. Such columns in the Shrine of Ibrāhīm and in the Chhoṭī Masjid have the uppermost register enriched with bead decorations, but elsewhere this register is undecorated. In all cases the bases are square, their four sides being ornamented with an Indian triangular pattern. The capitals are cushion shaped and surmounted by antecapitals, the brackets of which support the lintels. These are all devices conforming entirely to Indian traditions.

The constructional methods and the decorative designs of these buildings indicate that they must have been built by local Indian craftsmen. The end result shows that these workers were not prevented by their Muslim patrons from following their own traditional styles and techniques. At the same time the Muslims also introduced certain Islamic features which were entirely new to India. These features include the Arab-type hypostyle plan of the Solahkhambī Masjid, the *miḥrābs* of both of the mosques and of the Shrine of Ibrāhīm, and in particular the use of semi-circular

---

and its flat roof may indicate a fairly early form of construction for the building, John Marshall reports that the tomb has been wholly reconstructed, and there is so far no other evidence to establish a firm date for the tomb. The local tradition claiming that the original tomb must have been built soon after the death of Shāh Yūsuf and sometime early in the second half of the 12th century remains speculative, as the earliest historical inscription of the building records that it was built at the time of the Sūrī sultan Islām Shāh in 955/1548-9. See: H.M. Kuraishī, Multān, its brief history and Persian and Arabic inscriptions, *Epigraphia Indo-Moslemica*, 1927-8, 7; J. Marshall, The monuments of Muslim India, *Cambridge History of India*, Cambridge, 1928, III, 598; M. Wheeler, *5,000 Years of Pakistan*, London, 1950, 66; P. Brown, *Indian Architecture (Islamic Period)*, Bombay, 1956, 33, pl. 22, fig. 2.

arches in all these *miḥrābs* as well as in some of the windows of the Chhoṭī Masjid. The use of semi-circular arches as structural elements seems, however, to be still unknown to Indian craftsmen. In Bhadreśvar the seeming arches are no more than a decorative feature made by hollowing out the underside of a single block of stone surmounting the *miḥrābs* and the windows. Their form derives from the architecture of the Arab lands of Syria and northern Africa, and never reappears in India. After the Ghurid conquest of Delhi the arches introduced into the Islamic architecture of the subcontinent were pointed in profile, a form which thereafter remained in the Indo-Muslim tradition. *Miḥrābs* with a semi-circular plan, however, remain more common in India. Although the Ghurid conquerors of Delhi introduced the rectangular form of the plan represented in the Quwwat al-Islām mosque in Delhi[107] and the mosques in Bayana[108] and Kaman,[109] they also used the semi-circular plan for the *miḥrābs* of the Aṛhaī din kā Jhoṅpṛā mosque at Ajmer[110] and the Shāhī Masjid in Khatu.[111] These two mosques are both situated in towns in central Rajasthan, where an earlier tradition of mosque building could have already existed amongst local Muslim communities before the Ghurid conquest. The form was soon abandoned in northern India, and there is no other example of a *miḥrāb* with semi-circular plan in that area from the time of Īltutmish (1211-36) onward, but in Gujarat, where the form had already been firmly established, it continued to appear in many buildings such as in the *jāmi'* mosques of Bharoch[112] and Cambay,[113] both dating from the late 13th and early 14th century. In the 15th and 16th century and during the period of the Sultanate of Gujarat, *miḥrābs* with angular plans gradually took the place of those of the older style, but the semi-circular plan continued to be seen in some of the *miḥrābs*, for example in the mosque of Bībī Achut Kukī in Ahmadabad.[114]

All the other characteristics of the monuments of Bhadreśvar, both Hindu and Muslim, are seen again in later Indo-Islamic buildings. The early mosques of the Delhi Sultanate, such as the Quwwat al-Islām mosque in Delhi, and Arhaī din kā Jhoṅpṛā in Ajmer, as well as the mosques in Bayana and Kaman, are built upon an Arab plan, reusing Hindu and Jain columns, lintels and roof slabs. In Delhi the screen wall of the mosque[115] designed by the Muslims incorporates all the varieties of Indian decoration which were previously seen in Bhadreśvar, such as garlands and the diamond motifs seen in the Shrine of Ibrāhīm and in the Chhoṭī Masjid.

Several conclusions arise from the study of the Muslim monuments of Bhadreśvar. First, the existence of influential Muslim mercantile communities of the Ismā'īlī persuasion living — and we may assume prospering — under the Chaulukyan kingdom of Gujarat, throws an interesting light on the social conditions of the day. Such settlements must have made their contribution to the genesis of the local Ismā'īlī communities prominent today in the cities of Gujarat and Sind. These communities, however, seem to have retained no traditions of their forebears' existence. From the strictly architectural point of view, a wider conclusion emerges. The influence of Indian elements in the Islamic architecture of the subcontinent has often been explained as the mere consequence of the reuse of material from Hindu and Jain temples that had in many cases been specifically demolished for this purpose. At Bhadreśvar, on the other hand, we see that workmen trained in the Indian tradition were being employed on the building projects of a Muslim community who were not in possession of local political power, and had learnt to accommodate the vernacular style to Muslim ritual requirements. We have seen that there is significant archaeological and historical evidence in western India for the existence of similar Muslim settlements nearly 200 years before the monuments of Bhadreśvar. It is natural to suppose that these Muslim communities would

[107] J.A. Page, *An Historical Memoir on the Qutb: Delhi*, MASI, XXII, 1926, pl. 2.

[108] M. Shokoohy and N.H. Shokoohy, The architecture of Baha al-din Tughrul in the region of Bayana, Rajasthan, *Muqarnas*, IV, 1987, 121-9; A. Cunningham, Report on a Tour in Eastern Rajputana in 1882-3, *ASIR*, XX, Calcutta, 1885, pl. 13.

[109] *Ibid.*, 54-60, pl. 11; Muqarnas, IV, 114-21; M. Shokoohy, *Rajasthan*, I, Corpus Inscriptionum Iranicarum, Part IV, XLIX, London, 1986, pl. 50.

[110] *Ibid.*, pl. 1.

[111] Z.A Desai, *Mosques of India*, New Delhi, 1971, 28; M. Shokoohy, *Rajasthan*, I, pl. 51.

[112] J. Burgess, *Muhammadan Architecture of Bharoch, Cambay, Dholka, Champanir and Mahmudabad in Gujarat*, ASWI, I, London, 1896, pl. 3.

[113] *Ibid.*, pl. 18.

[114] J. Burgess, *The Muhammadan Architecture of Ahmadabad*, i, ASWI, VII, London, 1900, pl. 77.

[115] Tatsuro Yamamoto, *Delhi*, I, Tokyo, 1967, pl. 3b; Percy Brown, *Indian Architecture (Islamic Period)*, Bombay, 1968, pl. 7, fig. 2.

all have had their local monuments built by Hindu craftsmen, even if the actual monuments only survive in very remote locations. It remains to determine how widely such settlements are likely to have been distributed, and how far they may have penetrated towards the interior of the country and the centres of subsequent Indo-Muslim sultanates, especially those of Delhi. The mosques of Bayana and Kaman in the region of Delhi, with their colonnaded Arab plans, could well owe their inspiration to the knowledge of such earlier predecessors, and to the existence of teams of Hindu stonemasons already familiar with the requirements of such work, and acquainted with an architectural idiom of which the monuments of Bhadreśvar are at the moment the only well preserved examples. However, the full vindication of such a theory, should it carry conviction, will need to await further research, in lesser-known areas and at the village level, to find connecting evidence which the concentration by scholars on the main centres and former sultanate capitals has so far overshadowed. Only then will it be possible to judge the full implications of the Bhadreśvar material.

Mehrdad Shokoohy and Natalie H. Shokoohy

APPENDIX: THE MOSQUE OF ABULQĀSIM B. ʿALĪ AL-ĪRAJĪ IN JUNAGADH, GUJARAT

The continuation of the architectural traditions apparent in Bhadreśvar may also be seen in the mosque of Abulqāsim b. ʿAlī al-Īrajī in Junagadh. This town is located at 21° 31′ north and 70° 36′ east, on the Surashtra peninsula in Gujarat.[116] While the mosque of al-Īrajī has not yet attracted the attention of scholars to the extent it deserves, the town is well known for its ancient history and monuments going back to the Buddhist period. A number of Buddhist caves in Junagadh were studied by James Burgess,[117] who also visited the mosque of al-Īrajī, but only referred to it as "an old Hindu or Jain temple converted to a mosque".[118] Junagadh is about two kilometres west of the Jain religious complex on Mount Girnār, some of the temples of which date back to the 12th century.[119] However, as we shall see, there is no reason to believe that the mosque of al-Īrajī was originally a temple. The layout and stonework indicate that it is a mosque, and it bears an Arabic inscription dated 685/1286-7. The epigraph was first published by Dr. Z.A. Desai,[120] who pointed out that the edifice was built as a mosque and that its inscription refers to its construction. However, Dr. Desai's report is concerned only with epigraphy, and the structure itself is not described.

The inscription (pls. 56-7) is in two lines, cut into the stonework on the exterior of the lintel of the central entrance to the prayer chamber.[121] The second line is arranged on either side of a central diamond motif similar to those already seen above the doors of the monuments in Bhadreśvar. The inscription reads:

line 1:

امر ببناء هذا المسجد المبارك الصّدر[121a] المفضل المعظّم المنعم
المويّد المكرّم ملك الصّدور و النّواخيذ[121b] عماد الحاجّ و الحرمين

line 2 right side:

عفيف الدّنيا و الدّين ابوالقاسم بن علىّ الايرجىّ راجيا من اللّه
رضوانه

line 2 left side:

تقبل اللّه منه و غفر له و لوالديه فى سنه خمس ثمانين و ستماية

Translation: "Ordered the construction of this blessed mosque the great learned chief, beneficent, divinely assisted, and generous, the chief of the merchants (*malik al-ṣudūr*), and the shipmasters, the pillar of the pilgrims (to Mecca), and (of) the two shrines,[122] modest in the world, and of religion, Abulqāsim b. ʿAlī al-Īrajī in the hope of God's paradise. May God accept it from him and pardon him and his parents. In the year six hundred and eighty five".

While the date is about a century and a half later than that of the Shrine of Ibrāhīm in Bhadreśvar, and nearly a century later than the Ghurid conquest of northern India, it is still prior to the take-over of Gujarat by the Delhi Sultanate. Junagadh is situated between Somnath and Bhadreśvar, and the *Āʾīn-i Akbarī* mentions that it was captured by Sultan

---

[116] *The Imperial Gazetteer of India*, Oxford, 1908, XIV, 238.

[117] J. Burgess, *Report on the Antiquities of Kaṭhhiawād and Kachh*, ASWI, II, London, 1876, 93-147.

[118] *Ibid.*, 141.

[119] *Ibid.*, 167.

[120] Z.A. Desai, Arabic Inscriptions of the Rajput period from Gujarat, *Epigraphia Indica, Arabic and Persian Supplement*, 1961, 18-19.

[121] Dr. Desai does not record the exact location of the inscription and mentions that it is only in one line.

[121a] The word *ṣadr* is familiar as a religious title used in India in the sultanate and Mughal periods. However, in the pre-sultanate inscriptions of the Gujarat coast the word usually means the head of the Muslim trading community, who always appears to have been the chief merchant of the town, but probably took the role of religious leader at the same time. This is particularly clear in the bilingual inscription of Nākhudā Fīrūz at Somnath, see p. 10. For other inscriptions see: *EIAPS*, 1961, 23; 1971, 58.

[121b] An unusual spelling for النَّوَاخِذ or النَّوَاخِذة, both of which forms have also been seen in the inscriptions of the pre-sultanate trading communities of the Gujarat coast, see *EIAPS*, 1961, 13, 23.

[122] A reference to the holy sanctuaries in the two cities of Mecca and Medina, or Mecca and Jerusalem.

Maḥmūd of Ghazna who built a fort there.[123] However, while earlier historians mention the destruction of many temples by Maḥmūd on his way to Somnath they do not record the conquest of Junagadh, nor is it likely that during his campaign Maḥmūd spent any time constructing forts in India. The reference in the *Ā'īn-i Akbarī* should therefore be regarded as conjectural, since the conquest of many towns in India is attributed to Maḥmūd.

Although Delhi was conquered by the army of the Ghurid Sultan Muḥammad b. Sām in 588/1192-3, the territory gained did not include Gujarat. Fourteen years before this date, in 574/1178-9 when Muḥammad b. Sām first decided to conquer India he had indeed marched towards Naharwāla, the capital of the Chaulukyan kingdom of Gujarat.[124] Bhimadeva II, the king of Gujarat, defeated the Muslim army and forced the sultan to withdraw. In 593/1196-7 Bhimadeva had to endure another battle with the Muslims, this time against Quṭb al-dīn Aybak[125] the Ghurid governor of Delhi who was the commander of Muḥammad b. Sām's army. Quṭb al-dīn defeated Bhimadeva and took over Naharwāla, but had to withdraw from Gujarat without having established his authority there,[126] and Junagadh, together with the rest of Gujarat, retained its independence for almost another century.

The Islamic conquest of Gujarat was finally effected in 698/1298-9, when an army of 'Alā al-dīn Khaljī[127] took over the area, and annexed Gujarat to the sultanate of Delhi. While some local chieftains continued to rule in Surashtra, they must have been under Muslim rule, as the inscriptions of the Khalji and Tughluq sultans found in the area[128] show that from the end of the 13th century there was effective Muslim control of Surashtra.

During the 13th century, in spite of the constant threat of invasion by the Muslims of Delhi, peaceful Islamic settlements appear to have continued under Hindu rule. The bi-lingual inscription from Somnath mentioned above (p. 10) dates from this period. It refers to a grant given to the Muslims by the local ruler Arjunadeva for them to build a mosque in A.H. 662 (V.E. 1320/A.D. 1263). The person responsible for the construction of the mosque was a sailor and ship owner known as Fīrūz b. Abū Ibrāhīm from the state of Hormuz, and in the Arabic version[129] the Muslim ruler to whom these sailors gave their allegiance is recorded as Abū Nuṣrat Maḥmūd b. Aḥmad. The Sultan of Delhi, Nāṣir al-dīn Maḥmūd b. Īltutmish is not mentioned. Fīrūz the ship owner is not the only Persian who appears to have been a person of some standing amongst the Muslim communities of Gujarat. In Bhadreśvar one of the tombstones[130] belongs to one Abu'l-faraj b. 'Alī, from Sīrāf, at that time one of the most important ports on the Iranian coast of the Persian Gulf. Another inscription[131] found in Cambay records the construction of a mosque by 'Alī b. Shāpūr in 615/1218-19. The name Shāpūr shows the Iranian origin of this personage. Other epitaphs[132] are to be found in Cambay belonging to Abi'l-maḥāsin b. Ardashīr al-Ahwī (d. 630/1232-3), Sharaf al-dīn Murtiḍā b. Muḥammad al-Istarābādī, and 'Alī b. Sālār b. 'Alī Yazdī. Amongst these epitaphs are some belonging to a family from Bam who lived in Cambay for several generations.[133] In the inscription of the mosque at Junagadh, Īraj, the name of a southern Iranian city near Ramhurmuz, or of the ancestor of Abulqāsim b. 'Alī is also an indication of the Iranian origin of our "chief of the merchants and the shipmasters" of the town. This suggests that the Muslim community in Junagadh, like many other similar settlements in the other towns of Surashtra, had a strong and long established link with southern Iran, through the old commercial sea routes, and was unaffiliated to the Khurasani conquerors of northern

[123] Abu'l-faḍl 'Allāmī b. Shaykh Mubārak Nāgūrī, *'A'īn-i Akbarī*, ed. Blochmann, I, Calcutta, 1872, 489.

[124] Abū 'Umar Minhāj al-dīn 'Uthmān b. Sirāj al-dīn al-Jawzjānī, *Ṭabaqāt-i Nāṣirī*, Calcutta, 1864, 116.

[125] *Ibid.*, 140.

[126] G. Bühler, Eleven land-grants of the Chaulukyas of Anhilvād, *Indian Antiquary*, VI, 1877, 190-213; H.H. Dhruva, Sanskrit grants and inscriptions of Gujarāt kings; *ibid.*, XI, 1882, 99-101, W. Cartellieri, An Ābu inscription of the reign of Bhīmadeva II, dated Samvat 1265; *ibid.*, 220-3.

[127] Ḍiyā' al-dīn Barnī, *Tārīkh-i Fīrūz Shāhī*, Calcutta, 1862, 251; Yaḥyā b. Aḥmad b. 'Abdullāh al-Sihrindī, *Tārīkh-i Mubārak Shāhī*, Calcutta, 1931, 76.

[128] G. Yazdani, Inscriptions of the Khalji Sultans of Delhi, *Epigraphia Indo-Moslemica*, 1917-18, 32-3 and 37-8; also see *ibid.*, 1913-14, 29-30; *Epigraphia Indica, Arabic and Persian Supplement*, 1957-8, 38-9; 1962, 23-4, 27-30.

[129] Z.A. Desai, Arabic inscriptions of the Rajput period from Gujarat, 12-15.

[130] Present report, Part 2, tomb no. 2.

[131] Z.A. Desai, Arabic inscriptions of the Rajput period from Gujarat, 6-7.

[132] *Ibid.*, 1-24.

[133] Z.A. Desai, Some fourteenth century epitaphs from Cambay in Gujarat, *Epigraphia Indica, Arabic and Persian Supplement*, 1971, 6.

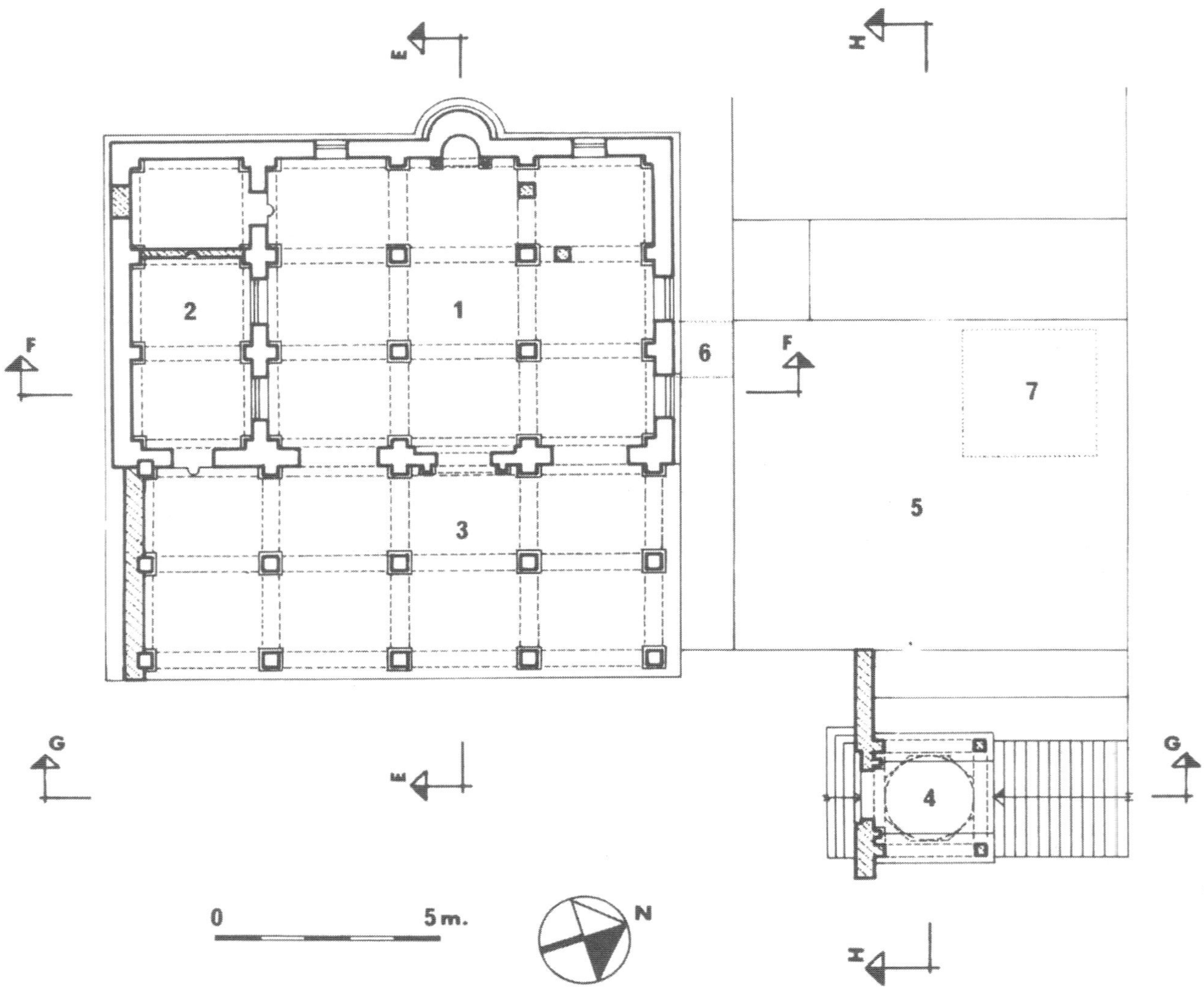

Fig. 36 Junagadh, the Mosque of al-Īrajī, site plan. 1: prayer hall; 2: secondary chamber; 3: portico; 4: northern gateway; 5: lower courtyard in front of Bhuddist cave; 6: domed pavilion attached to mosque; 7: domed pavilion in courtyard of cave.

India in the 13th century who were of Turkish or north Iranian origin.

The mosque (figs. 36-41, pls. 48-57) is situated on the outskirts of the present town of Junagadh,[134] north of the ancient fort of Uparkot to the north-east of the town. It is in a rocky area with many ancient caves. The area is known as Māī Gaḍechī, and is near the site of the Dhārāgaḍh, the old northern gate of the town. Apart from the mosque of al-Īrajī there is a later mosque, a shrine, a number of tombs, and a step well. Unlike the mosques of Bhadreśvar, the mosque of al-Īrajī is still in use, and other structures have been put up around it. They include two domed pavilions (fig. 36, nos. 6 and 7 in plan) and a gateway (no. 4 in plan) to the north of the present courtyard. The mosque itself is built on a platform set on solid rock. On the northern side the rock has been cut back, and

[134] J. Burgess, *Memorandum on the Antiquities at Dabhoi etc.*, ASWI, II, 1875, 9-16; J. Burgess, *Report on the Antiquities of Kaṭhiawād and Kachh*, ASWI, London, 1876, 94, 143-4; *ASIAR*, 1921, 2-18; *Epigraphia Indica, Arabic and Persian Supplement*, 1953-4, 62-70.

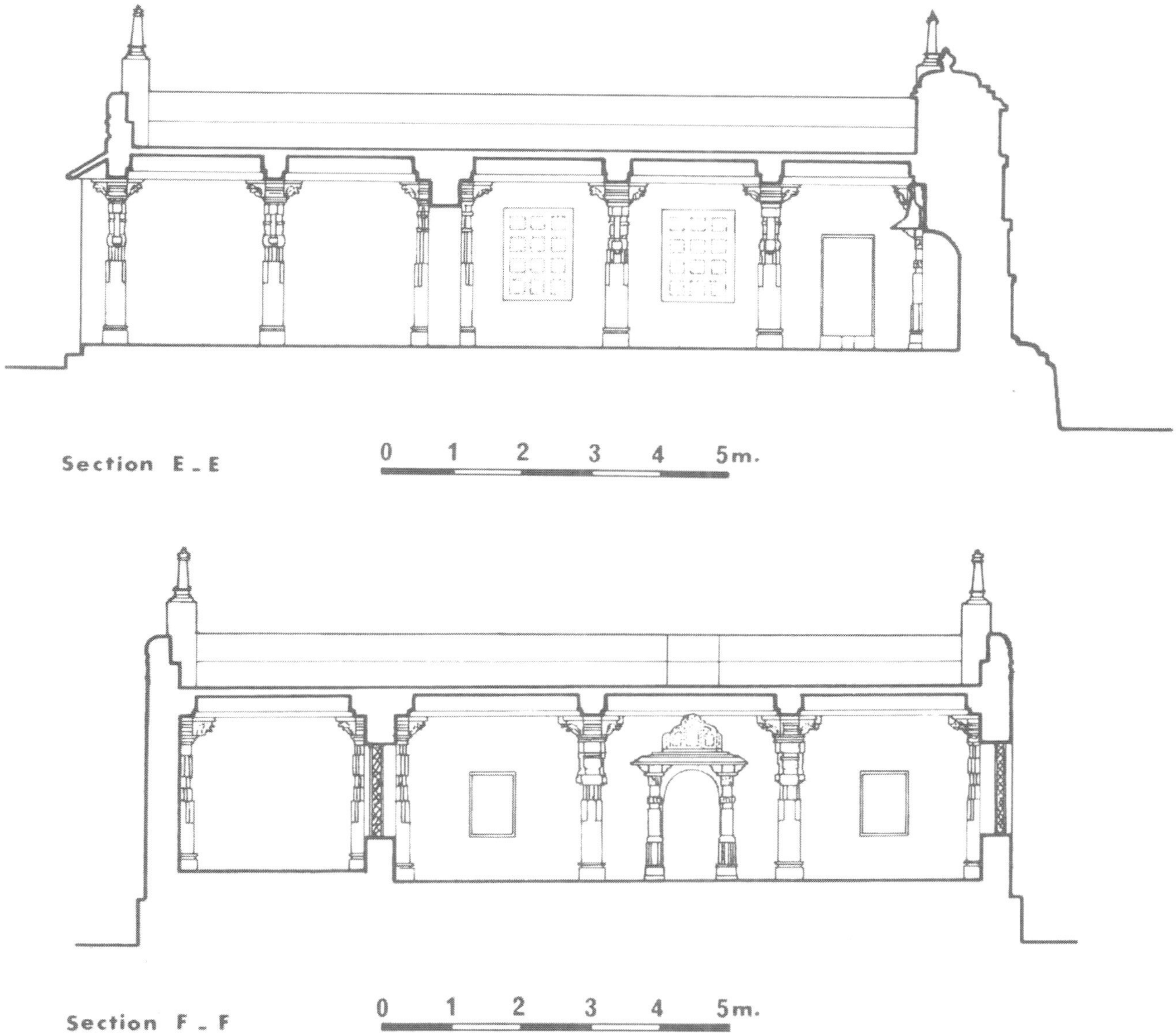

Fig. 37 The Mosque of al-Īrajī, section E-E through the mosque and the portico, and section F-F through the sanctuary and the southern chamber.

below the mosque on this side is the excavated cave (fig. 39, pl. 49a) already studied by Burgess. It has columns carved out of the rock forming a chamber three bays wide and two aisles deep leading to a small underground cell on the east of the chamber. The chamber is now regarded as an Islamic shrine, but its origin is not known. There are a number of Buddhist caves nearby, and in the Uparkot some Buddhist monasteries have been excavated several stories deep into the rock. The cave below the mosque of al-Īrajī may therefore be of Buddhist origin.

The mosque consists of a main sanctuary chamber (no. 1 in plan) with another long and narrow chamber (no. 2) to the south and a large colonnaded portico (no. 3) to the east. There is a courtyard to the east of the portico, but its original enclosure no longer

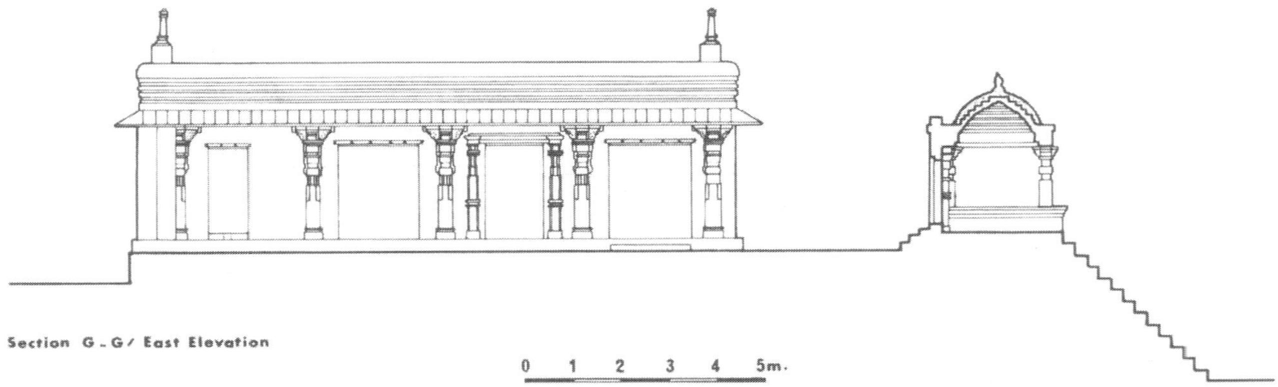

Fig. 38 The Mosque of al-Īrajī, section G-G through the courtyard and the northern gateway, showing the eastern façade of the mosque.

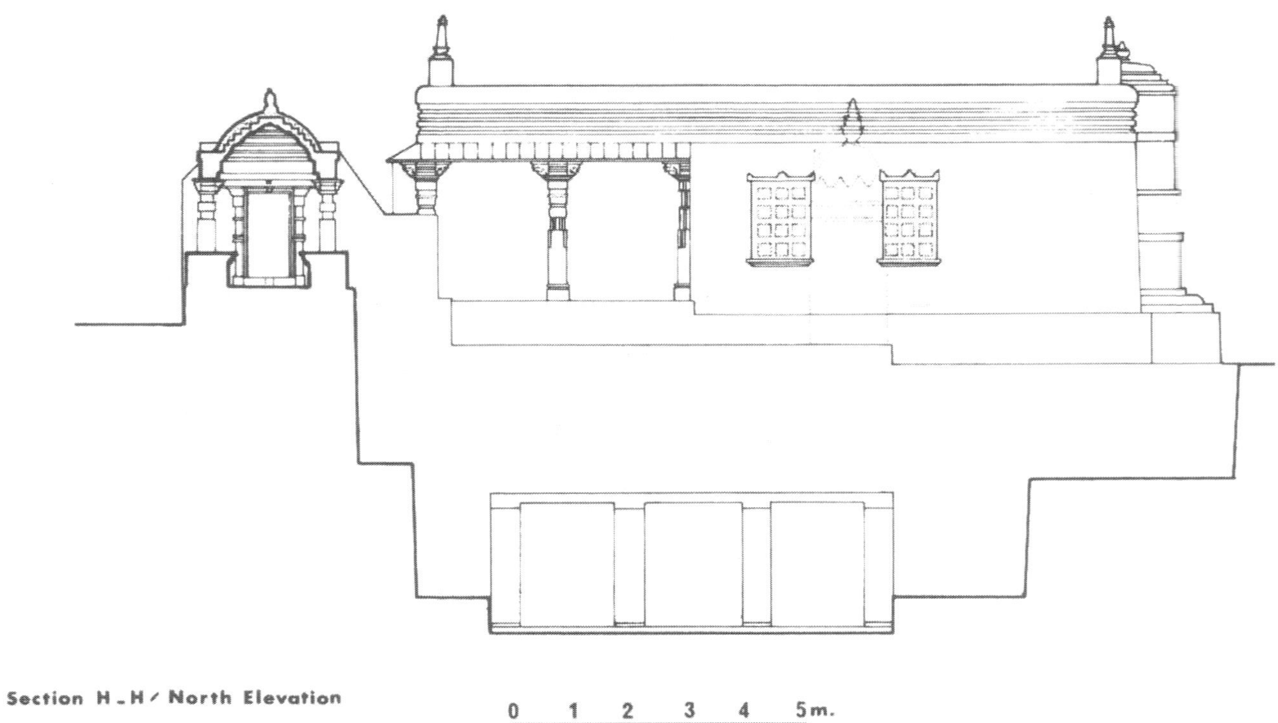

Fig. 39 The Mosque of al-Īrajī, section H-H through the northern gateway and courtyard 5 outside the mosque, showing the northern façade of the ancient cave and the mosque.

survives, and its present walls are of later dates. This courtyard is not shown in the plan. Like the mosques of Bhadreśvar, the mosque of al-Īrajī is built of large blocks of stone with monolithic lintels and shafts for the columns and pilasters. The roof consists of flat slabs resting on lintels supported by brackets and ante-capitals. Around the roof is a parapet built with four courses of stone (fig. 40). The first course is decorated with rows of diamonds and has stone water spouts, and the top course is carved to form a drip stone.

The sanctuary chamber of the mosque (pls. 54a and 55a) is three bays wide and three aisles deep, with four columns in the chamber, and corresponding

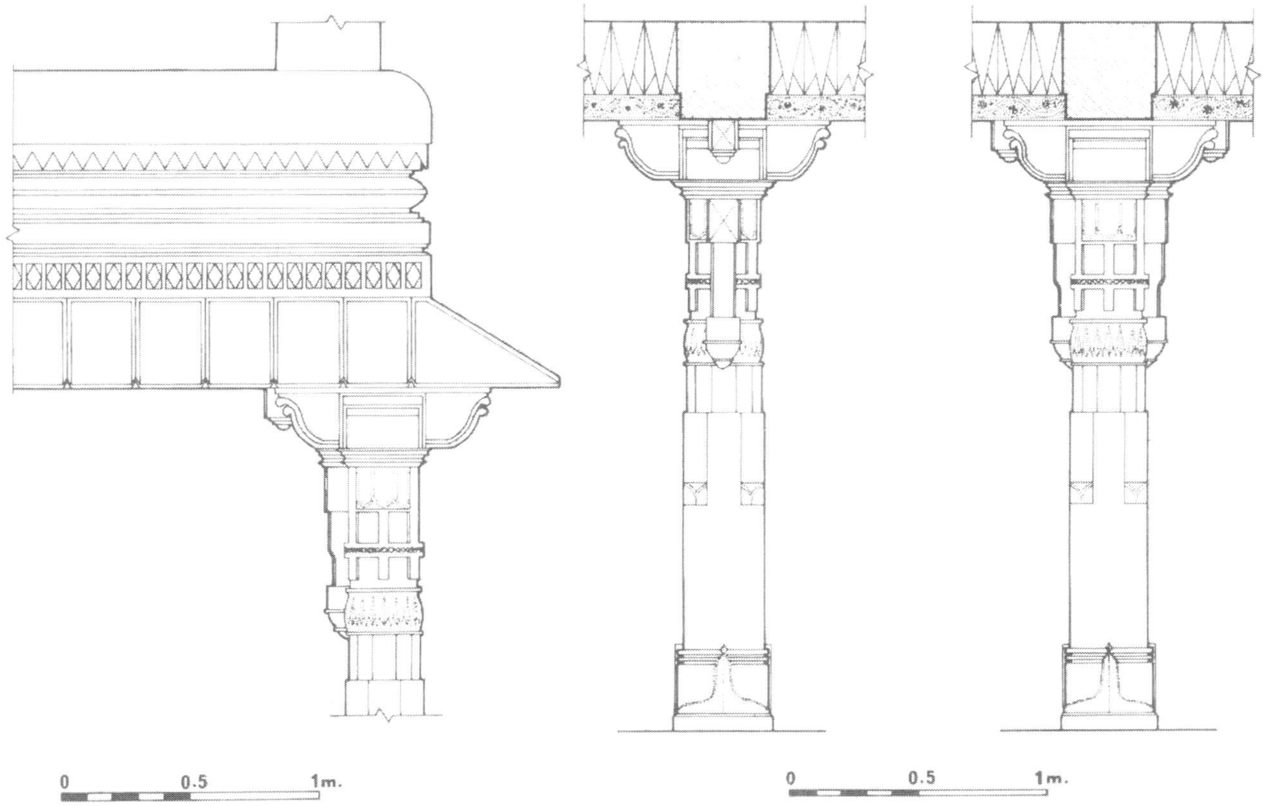

Fig. 40 The Mosque of al-Īrajī, details of the stonework of the portico and of a column.

pilasters set into walls. The single *miḥrāb* (fig. 37, pl. 53b) is in the middle of the western wall of this chamber. It is semi-circular in plan, and its projection outside is also semi-circular (pl. 51a). Like the *miḥrābs* in Bhadreśvar, it has a semi-circular arch. Framing the *miḥrāb* are two columns supporting a carved lintel set on brackets. Above the lintel is a slab of stone carved in relief to represent three arches. The columns and the slabs are not attached to the wall, and as their decoration differs from that of the rest of the building it seems that they must be of a later date. No trace of any earlier decoration remains in the *miḥrāb*, and there are no slots in the stonework as are seen in the *miḥrābs* at Bhadreśvar. The projection of the *miḥrāb* on the exterior has a decorative solid dome (pl. 50a) at the level of the roof of the mosque.

The sanctuary has two windows on the northern and on the southern side, and a window on either side of the *miḥrāb* (figs. 37, 39, pls. 48b, 54, 55b). These all have pierced stonework, and have architraves and sills on the outside, but are plain on the inside. On the eastern side the sanctuary has three doors opening to a portico (fig. 38, pls. 49b, 55a). The dated inscription is on the lintel of the central doorway, and is carved on the side facing the portico. It seems that the two entrances to the sanctuary on either side of the central opening were at some time enlarged, as they are now broader and higher than the central entrance, and lack pilasters. The portico (pls. 48, 49b and 52b) has two rows of free-standing columns and corresponding pilasters on the exterior wall of the sanctuary. The portico's southern side is walled, but the wall may be of a later date. The north and east side of the roof of the portico is provided with eavestones, set below the parapet, and supported by stub lintels resting on the front brackets of the ante-capitals (fig. 40).

On the southern side of the sanctuary is a secluded chamber (no. 2 in plan, pl. 54b) with a door on the east opening to the portico, and another to the western aisle of the sanctuary. There is a third door to the

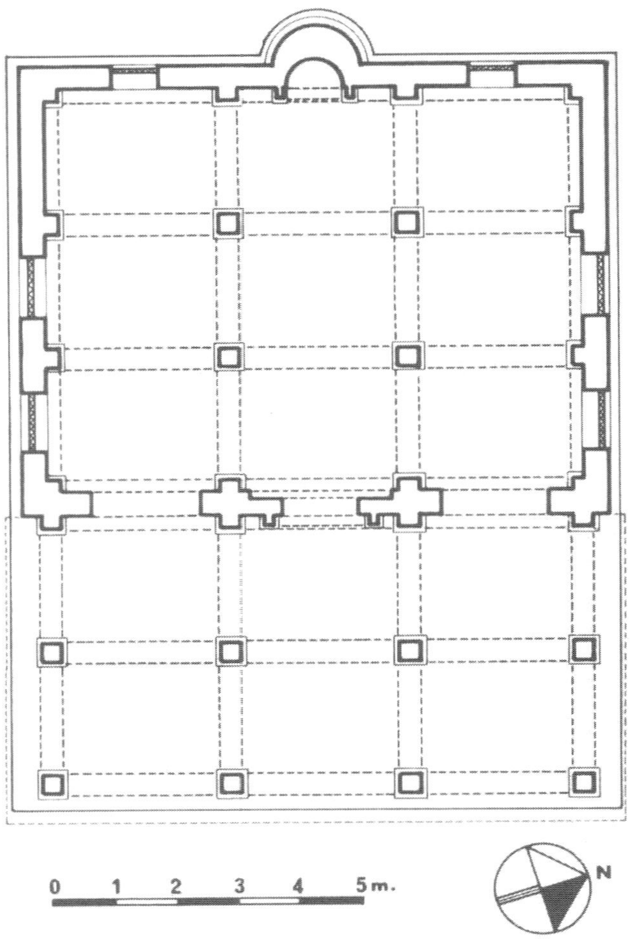

Fig. 41 The Mosque of al-Īrajī, plan of the building in its original state.

outside (pl. 50a), now blocked, opposite the door to the sanctuary. We may assume that the original function of the chamber was to provide a private area for women, but it has recently been divided into two and is used as a store-room. However, the whole of the southern chamber appears to be a later addition to the mosque as the two windows (pls. 54a and 55b) between the sanctuary and this chamber are provided with sills and projecting architraves to throw off rain water, matching those of the other windows of the mosque (pl. 48b). This would indicate that it was once an exterior wall. The portico in front of the chamber must have been extended by one bay. The carving of the lintels and of the parapet matches that of the main building, and the pilasters follow the design of the rest of the mosque, but vary in their decorative details. The similarity of the stonework of the extension with that of the main building may be an indication that the mosque was enlarged fairly soon after it was first built. The original mosque, therefore, would have consisted only of the sanctuary with a single *miḥrāb* in the middle of the *qibla* wall, and a portico at the eastern side (fig. 41). A symmetrical layout of this kind, based on a central axis, is usual in the monuments of this period.

The decoration of the lintels (fig. 40, pl. 55a) of the mosque is closely comparable with that of Bhadreśvar. The lintels are divided into two horizontal registers, the lower one with the usual garland pattern, and the upper with a row of diamonds and darts. On the soffits of the lintels are carved lotuses, similar to those of the Shrine of Ibrāhīm and the Chhoṭī Masjid. The columns (fig. 40, pl. 52b) are, however, more elaborately decorated than at Bhadreśvar. The shafts are divided into four registers, square at the base, then octagonal, sixteen sided, and round. The lower part of the circular register represents a half opened lotus, above which are carved strings of beads and rings of diamonds and discs. The circular registers have flanges on either side giving support to two of the brackets of the ante-capitals. The columns are arranged so that these flanges are on a north-south axis.

To the north of the courtyard of the mosque is a gateway in the form of a chatri (fig. 36, no. 4 on plan, and 38-39, pl. 51b and 52a) reached by a flight of steps. The chatri is roofed with a corbelled dome, and is of considerable age, but as the details of the decoration of its columns and lintels differ from those of the mosque it may not be contemporary with the mosque.

To the eastern side of the mosque and probably within the original courtyard a step-well (pl. 58) has been excavated into the solid rock. The upper part is lined with blocks of stone, but the well is unornamented, and has no platform or building above it. There is an arch, probably built to consolidate the upper part of the well. This arch seems to be a relatively recent addition.

Other later additions to the complex are a small domed chamber (no. 6 on plan, pl. 48b) attached to the north wall of the mosque, and a free standing square domed tomb chamber (no. 7 on plan, pls. 48b and 49a) standing in the courtyard (no. 5) on the level of the excavated cave. Burgess[135] suggests that this may have been part of an ancient garden perhaps connected with a bath.

The Mosque of al-Īrajī, dating almost a century and a half after the Islamic monuments of Bhadreśvar, shows how much the layout and decoration of the pre-conquest mosques of Bhadreśvar had become the established pattern along the coast and also inland in Gujarat. Soon after the construction of this mosque the Khaljī take-over of Gujarat brought a long period of Islamic domination. A great number of important mosques have survived in the area. Although they follow the general principles seen in the Bhadreśvar mosques, none of the sultanate mosques in Gujarat has a portico. This feature was not usual in mosque architecture, and as we have seen was probably adopted by the Muslim settlers from the architecture of Indian temples, but it appears that the conquerors did not favour this arrangement. The semi-circular plan for the *miḥrāb* remains as a feature of many Indian mosques, and projecting the back wall becomes established practice. In the sultanate mosques, however, pointed arches were adopted in place of semi-circular arches for the *miḥrābs*.

---

[135] J. Burgess, *Report on the Antiquities of Kaṭhiawād and Kachh*, ASWI, 1874-5, 141.

PART TWO

A STUDY OF THE ISLAMIC INSCRIPTIONS IN BHADREŚVAR

Manijeh Bayani-Wolpert

A STUDY OF THE ISLAMIC INSCRIPTIONS IN BHADREŚVAR

THE SHRINE OF IBRĀHĪM

The inscriptions of Bhadreśvar were first published in 1965 by Dr. Z.A. Desai, who mentioned their importance in the study of the history of Muslim Gujarat in that they include the earliest dated example of an Islamic monumental inscription in India.[1] My reading of these inscriptions differs from that of Dr. Desai only in a few words of the historical text, in the inscription above the western window at the northern side[2] (pl. 5a) of the shrine, and in a few words on the tombstones. In addition, it may be worth re-examining these inscriptions in the hope of discovering more about their historical significance from their calligraphic style.

This building is referred to here as the Shrine of Ibrāhīm (fig. 42, pls. 64-5) after Dr. Desai's reading of the inscriptions.[3] Although the presence of a *miḥrāb*, the surrounding graveyard, and the use of the Throne Verse all point to a religious function, probably funerary, such a conclusion is not immediately obvious from the inscription carved in relief on the frieze of the portico. Parts of the inscriptions are not clear, and my reading, which differs from Dr. Desai's, depends on some grammatical and contextual assumptions. The sentence in question begins with the clearly decipherable word *hādhā*, and later on the northern wall continues with the equally clear *al-'abd al-ḍa'īf al-rājī bi raḥmat allāh*. What is written between these is the subject of this difference in reading. The word *hādhā* can be followed by either a noun or a clause. If it were a noun, such as for example "grave" (as Dr. Desai suggests), it should, like the words following it, take the definite article *al*. There is no doubt that whatever this section does begin with, it is definitely not *al*, and if therefore the word were merely *qabr* it should be followed by the name of the deceased, and not the words *al-'abd*, etc.[4] Another sequence which could follow *hādhā* is a clause beginning with a word such as *mā* "what" or *mimmā* "one of what". The double *mīm* and the *alif* seem fairly distinguishable and therefore suggest that the word following *hādhā* is indeed *mimmā*. This in turn is followed by two words, one above *mimmā*, and a shorter word after it. The word *mimmā* can only be followed by a phrase or a verb such as: *amara bi-banā'ihi* (or *'imāratihi*) "ordered its construction" or *'umila* "made" or *'umira* "constructed". The word squeezed in above *mimmā* could be read as *amara* "ordered" or *'umira* "constructed", but the following word is not legible. However, if it is the former, it can either be a word denoting its construction such as *bi-'inshā'ihi* "its erection", *bi-banā'ihi* "its construction", *bi-tajdīdihi* "its renovation", or *bi-'imāratihi* "its construction", or just *bihi* "to it" which might be the most likely word because of the short space.

The inscription then continues "the weak servant, hoping for the mercy[5] of God, Ibrāhīm, son of Abu'l-Futūḥ...in the date of...". What appears between the name and the date is not very clear; however, certain letters can be read clearly, such as *dāl* or *dhāl* followed

---

[1] Z.A. Desai, Kūfī epitaphs from Bhadreśwar in Gujarat, *Epigraphia Indica, Arabic and Persian Supplement*, 1965, 1-8.

[2] Dr. Desai called these windows "doors".

[3] Dr. Desai gives the following reading:

بسم الله الرحمن الرحيم صلى الله على النبـى و آله ... هذا قبر(؟) / العبد الضعيف
الراجى الى رحمة الله ابراهيم بن ابو العزم / عبد الله (؟) بن بكر(؟) ... توفى الى الله
بتاريخ (؟) ذى الحجه لسنه اربعه و خمسين و خمسمائه /

"In the name of Allah, the Beneficent, the Merciful. Blessing of Allah be upon the Prophet Muḥammad and his descendants .../of the great. This grave is of / the weak creature, hopeful of the mercy of Allah, Ibrāhīm, son of Abu'l-'Aẓm/'Abdullāh (?), son of Bakr (?) ... was taken into the mercy of Allah in the month of *dhi'l-ḥijja* of the year (A.H.) four and fifty and five hundred (*dhi'l-ḥijja* A.H. 554/December 1159–January 1160 A.D.).

[4] There are examples where this rule is not observed, as in Tombs nos. 2 and 3; also see Et. Combe, J. Sauvaget, G. Wiet, *Répertoire chronologique d'épigraphie arabe*, XI, Cairo, 1942, 71 and 138, both belonging to the mid 7th/13th century, from Petland and Damascus.

[5] Dr. Desai read this part as *al-rājī ilā raḥmat allāh*, "hopeful of the mercy of Allah".

Fig. 42 Bhadreśvar, inscriptions of the Shrine of Ibrāhīm.

by *'ain* or *ghain* at the beginning of the next line, followed in turn by a few undeciphered letters, and ending with the letters *rā* or *zā* and *alif*. What is clear is that this section of the inscription does not contain the word "died" as claimed by Dr. Desai. It would appear, therefore that this inscription does not refer to the tomb of Ibrāhīm who died in 554/1159-60, but to the building which he had ordered to be constructed in that year. Furthermore, since the word *mimmā* occurs, it strongly suggests that there were other buildings ordered by Ibrāhīm, and so we are probably dealing with a person of some standing.

The identity of this personage is not known. The only well-known figure who might be our Ibrāhīm is Ibrāhīm ibn al-Ḥusain al-Ḥāmidī, who became *dā'ī muṭlaq* of the Yemen and its neighbourhood, as well as India and Sind in the year 536/1141, with his headquarters in Ṣan'ā.[6] As far as the name Abu'l Futūḥ is concerned, we know that at the time of Maḥmūd's invasion of Multan in 401/1010-11, the Ismā'īlī *dā'ī* was Abu'l-Futūḥ Dāwūd ibn Naṣr, who was taken prisoner, and died in Ghazna.[7] If our Ibrāhīm is connected with this Abu'l-Futūḥ, the gap of about 150 years between their dates means that the latter must have been the former's grandfather or great-grandfather, and if this is so, the names of the intermediate generation(s) have been omitted. The fact that the name is given as Ibrāhīm ibn Abu'l-Futūḥ, instead of Abi'l-Futūḥ may be because it refers to Ibrāhīm the son of the Abu'l-Futūḥ branch. The interesting point is that both Ibrāhīm and Abu'l-Futūḥ are related to the Ismā'īlī sect and as is mentioned in the historical background (page 9) a mosque was built for the *Shimalī*, which is suggested by Bühler to mean the Ismā'īlī community. The only reference in our inscription which might confirm the Ismā'īlī connection with this building is the phrase: "May God bless the Prophet Muḥammad, and his family". Although the inclusion of Muḥammad's family in a blessing was not an exclusively *shī'a* practice, its use does become more common under the Fatimids. Thus the appearance of *ālihi*, "his family", might be the reflection of Fatimid influence in Bhadreśvar.

The inscription reads:

[بسـ]م الله الرحمن الرحيم صلى الله على النبـى محمد و آله
[وسلم؟] الله لا اله الا هو الحى القيوم لا تاخذه سنه و لا نوم
[له] ما فى السـ[موا]ت وما فى الارض من / ذالذى يشفع عنده
الا باذنه يعلم ما بين ايد / يهم وما خلفهم و لا يحيطون بشى من
علمه الا بما شا وسع كرسيه السموات و الارض و لا يووده

[6] H.F. Al-Hamdani, H.S.M. Al-Juhni, *Aṣ-ṣulayḥīyūn wa'l-ḥarakat al-fāṭimīyya fi'l-Yaman*, Cairo, 1305 A.H. (1887-8), 270.

[7] Abbas Husain Al-Hamdani, *Ismā'īlī Da'wā: the Beginning of the Ismā'īlī Da'wā in Northern India*, Cairo, 1956, 4.

حفظهما و هو العلى العظيم هذا مما امر [به؟] / العبد الضعيف
الراج[ـى] برحمة الله ابرهيم بن ابو الفتوح / دع؟ .... را فى
تاريخ شهر الله الا [خر؟] ذى حجه سنه اربعه و خمسين و
خمسمائه /.

"In the name of God, the Compassionate, the Merciful. May God bless the Prophet Muḥammad and his family and grant him salvation (followed by *Qur'ān*, II, 255). This is one of what the weak servant, hoping for the mercy of God, Ibrāhīm, son of Abu'l-Futūḥ ... ordered in the date of the holy month, the end of [?] *dhī ḥijja* (sic), in the year five hundred and fifty four (January 1160 A.D.)."

Other inscriptions of the shrine are carved in relief on the lintels above the western windows at the northern and the southern sides (fig. 42, last two lines). The inscription above the western window at the southern side (pl. 5b) reads:

سلام عليكم طبتم فادخلوها خالدين

(*Qur'ān*, XXXIX, 73).

The inscription above the window at the northern side (pl. 5a) reads:

و من دخله كان آمنا و لله على الناس

(*Qur'ān*, III, 96).[8]

The use of this verse is common on mosques and shrines, but it is most appropriate for this building since the house which is referred to is meant to be the Place of Abraham in Mecca, and, as we have seen, this building was built by a certain Abraham (Ibrāhīm). There is no doubt that this phrase would be more appropriate if this were really the shrine of Ibrāhīm himself.

There are three mistakes in the historical inscription, of the type usually attributed to non-Arabs. The first is in the name Ibrāhīm ibn Abu'l-Futūḥ. If Ibrāhīm was the son, the correct form should be Ibrāhīm ibn Abi'l-Futūḥ. The second is in the month *dhī'l-ḥijja* which appears here as *dhī ḥijja*, and the third is in the phrase *al-rājī bi-raḥmat allāh* which should be *al-rājī ilā raḥmat allāh*. However, since mistakes are found even in inscriptions written by Arabs,[9] on this basis alone it cannot be assumed that it was written by a non-Arab hand. In addition, as we shall see, the calligraphic style of the inscription is connected with the work of Arabs or with that of the Arab-speaking people of North Africa.

THE STYLE OF WRITING

The calligraphic style with foliation, lobed ending of letters, and scroll and floral decoration either in the background or attached to letters falls in the group known as "floriated Kufic". The inscription is clearly written, and at times a word or a letter is written above the base line of the main inscription, either on the same scale or smaller. The letters are sometimes elongated to reach the upper border, and are normally joined to the preceding ones by loops below the base line of the lettering. The endings of letters are executed in various ways from simple to wedge-shaped, lobed, foliated, swan-neck (facing left or right), straight, with or without an additional horizontal stroke or broken into an arch form, always pointed to the left (except in one case in the word *bi-shaī'*), and overlapping, However, the most distinctive features of this style are the use of a horizontal tail for a vertical stroke, the breaking of an upright tail of a letter into an arch form, and overlapping. The first of these are found on inscriptions from various parts of the Islamic world. In eastern Islam it is found on the inscriptions from Ghazna,[10] Lashkarī Bāzār,[11] and on the

[8] This was read by Dr. Desai as: "and from every place (we have brought forth a) nation. And to Allah".

[9] Samuel Flury, *Islamische Schriftbander Amida-Diarbekr, XI Jahrhundert, Anhang Kairuan-Mayyāfāriqīn-Tirmidh*, Basel-Paris, 1920, 36, and footnote no. 4; Evariste Levi-Provençal, *Inscriptions arabes d'Espagne*. Leiden - Paris, 1931, Introduction, 26-8; R. Ettinghausen, Arabic Epigraphy: Communication or Symbolic Affirmation, *Studies in Honour of George C. Miles*, American University of Beyrut, 1974, 297-317.

[10] A. Bombaci, *The Kufic Inscriptions in Persian Verses in the Court of the Royal Palace of Mas'ūd III at Ghazni*, Instituto Italiano per il Medio ed Estremo Oriente, Rome, 1966, pl. 32, no. 10 i, pl. 33, nos. 11c, 14a-c; pl. 34, no. 17e. Also: S. Flury, *Ghazni, le décor épigraphique des monuments de Ghazna*, Paris, 1925, pl. 7, nos. 12 and 18; pl. 12, nos. 7, 8, 11.

[11] Janine Sourdel-Thomine, *Lashkari Bazar, une résidence royale ghaznévide et ghoride, le décor non-figuratif et les inscriptions*, Mémoires de la Délegation Archéologique Française en Afghanistan, XVIII, part 1B, Paris, 1978, pl. 135, nos. 14 and 18.

inscriptions from Amida in Diarbekr[12] where, however, it is less pronounced. In western Islam it is found at Qairawān on the *maqṣūra* of Sidi ʿUqbā,[13] on the Bāb Tūnis,[14] and on tombstones.[15] It appears also on inscriptions found in Qalʿa Banū Ḥammād in Algeria,[16] and on tombstones from Sicily.[17] This feature is also common on inscriptions in Egypt belonging to the 6th/12th century, in the mosque of Ṣāliḥ Ṭalāʾī,[18] and on the wood carvings in the tombs of al-Shabīhī[19] and Imām Shāfiʿī,[20] as well as on other wood carvings now in the Museum of Islamic Art in Cairo.[21] A similar calligraphic feature is also found on the inscriptions of the Dhū Jibla mosque in the Yemen.[22]

The broken form into an arch facing left (as seen in letters *mīm* and *nūn* of the opening formula) is only found on the inscriptions from western Islam, on various tombstones from Qairawān[23], the *maqṣūra* of Sidi ʿUqbā,[24] Bāb Tūnis[25] (both in Qairawān), on the inscriptions from Qalʿa Banū Ḥammād,[26] as well as on stone fragments from Tunisia.[27] The only example of this practice outside Tunisia is found on a tombstone from Sicily which was clearly influenced by a Tunisian prototype.[28] It should be noted that broken forms of letters are found in other parts of the Islamic world, but the letters are all broken in the upper part of the tail to the right,[29] rather than in the lower part to the left (fig. 42, letter *mīm* in the word *bism*).

The most distinctive characteristic of this style is, however, the overlapping of letters as they appear in the words: *al-raḥmān, al-raḥīm, dhī ḥijja, wa man, dakhalahu, fa adkhulūhā*, and *khālidīn*. This practice is mainly found in Tunisian inscriptions: on tombstones dated 429/1038,[30] 434/1042,[31] 43?/1039-48,[32] 440/1048-9,[33] 496/1102,[34] 515/1121,[35] 534/1139,[36] 535/1140,[37] and on an undated tombstone of the same period.[38] The only example of a similar practice outside Tunisia is on a tombstone from Sicily dated 531/1137,[39] on the Rādkān tower dated 411/1020-21,[40] and in Dhū Jibla mosque in the Yemen (though not identical),[41] and on an unglazed jar in the Louvre attributed by Flury to 12th century Iran.[42]

---

[12] Flury, *Amida-Diarbekr*, pl. 6 nos 1 and 12; pl. 4 nos. 1, 12 and 18; pl. 8 nos. 1 and 12.

[13] *Ibid.*, pl. 15, nos. 5, 12-14, 16-18.

[14] A. Grohmann, The origin and early development of floriated Kufic, *Ars Orientalis*, II, 1957, 183-213, fig. 23.

[15] M. El-Habib, Stèles funéraires kairouanaises du IIIᵉ/IXᵉ au Vᵉ/XIᵉ siècles, Etude typologique et esthétique, *Revue des études Islamiques*, XLIII, Paris 1975, fig. 18 no. 41b; fig. 34, no. 21a; fig. 37, no. 41a; fig. 39 no. 21d; fig. 42 no. 14b; A. S. Arif, *Arabic Lapidary Kufic in Africa, Egypt-North Africa-Sudan*, London, 1967, 18, 22, 59, 65, 74, 102 and 114.

[16] L. de Beyle, *La Kalaa des Bani-Hammad, une capitale berbère de l'Afrique du Nord au XIᵉ siècle*, Paris, 1909, ch. 3, pl. 29.

[17] M. Amari, *Le epigrafi di Sicilia*, Palermo, (s.a.), pl. 3.

[18] K.A.C. Creswell, *Muslim Architecture of Egypt*, I, Oxford, 1952, pl. 97d.

[19] These inscriptions are unpublished.

[20] K.A.C. Creswell, *Muslim Architecture of Egypt*, II, Oxford, 1959, pl. 26c.

[21] On the *miḥrāb* of Sayida Nafīsa (532-41/1138-46), see J. David-Weill, *Catalogue général du musée arabe du Caire: les bois à épigraphes jusqu'à l'époque mamluke*, Cairo, 1931, pl. 14 no. 421: on an inscription dated 541/1146-7, pl. 15 no. 4138. For other examples see: pl. 18 no. 3100; pl. 19, nos. 2409 and 2410; pl. 20 no. 646.

[22] R. Lewcock and G.R. Smith, Two early mosques in the Yemen: a preliminary report, *Art and Archaeology Research Papers*, IV, December, 1973, 117-130, pl. 12.

[23] B. Roy and P. Poinssot, *Inscriptions arabes de Kairouan*, Publications de l'Institut des hautes etudes de Tunis, II, fasc. I, Paris 1950, pl. 35 no. 211, 5; pl. 36 no. 211, 13, 14, 16; pl. 42 no. 233, 5, 14, 16; II, fasc. II, Paris, 1958, pl. 65 no. 429, 5; pl. 66 no. 429, 11, 14, 16; pl. 77 no. 503, 16, 17; pl. 79 no. 519, 5; pl. 80 no. 519, 14, 16; El-Habib, *Stèles funéraires*, figs. 21 no. 65a; 22 no. 41b; 29 no. 65c; 32 no. 41; 34 no. 41; 39 no. 41a.

[24] Flury, *Amida-Diarbekr*, pl. 15.

[25] Grohmann, Floriated Kufic, fig. 23.

[26] De Beyle, *La Kalaa des Bani-Hammad*, ch. 3, pl. 29; Lucien Golvin, *Recherches archéologiques à la Qal'a des Banū Hammād*, Paris, 1965, 170-180, figs. 61-6.

[27] S.M. Zbiss, *Corpus des inscriptions de Tunisie*, Notes et Documents, VIII, tom. 1, Tunis, 1955, pl. 12 no 20.

[28] M. Amari, *Le epigrafi di Sicilia*, pl. 3.

[29] On the inscribed wood carving of the tombs of Imām Shāfiʿī and Shabīhī (both in Cairo and unpublished); the inscriptions in Amida: Flury, *Amida-Diarbekr*, pls. 3, 4, 6, 8, 10; Imām Khurd in Afghanistan: A.D.H, Bivar, Seljuqid *zīyārats* of Sar-i Pul (Afghanistan), *Bulletin of the School of Oriental and African Studies, University of London*, XXIX, 1966, pls. 1 and 3-5; Rādkān: Flury, *Amida-Diarbekr*, pl. 14; on pottery from Nīshāpūr: L. Volov (Golombek), Plaited Kufic on Samanid epigraphic pottery, *Ars Orientalis*, VI, 1966, 107-33, 111; and the inscription of the Dhū Jibla Mosque in the Yemen: Lewcock and Smith, Two early mosques in the Yemen, pl. 12.

[30] Roy and Poinssot, *Inscriptions arabes de Kairouan*, *op. cit.*, II, fasc. II, pl. 51 in letters *fā* (or *qāf*) and *wāw*.

[31] *Ibid.*, pl. 59 in letters *wāw* and *nūn*.

[32] *Ibid.*, pl. 71 in the letter *wāw*.

[33] *Ibid.*, pl. 73 in the letter *wāw*.

[34] Zbiss, *Corpus*, pl. 22 no. 20 in the words *al-raḥmān* and *al-raḥīm*.

[35] *Ibid.*, pl. 34 no. 47 in the word *al-raḥmān*.

[36] *Ibid.*, pl. 38 no. 54 in the word *al-raḥmān*.

[37] Roy and Poinssot, *op. cit.*, II, fasc. II, pl. 91 in the letter *wāw*.

[38] Zbiss, *Corpus*, pl. 24 no. 25 in the word *khulūn*.

[39] Amari, *Le epigrafi di Sicilia*, pl. 7.

[40] Flury, *Amida-Diarbekr*, pl. 14 nos. 1o and p; 5f; 9a; 14g and h; 16e.

[41] Lewcock and Smith, Two early mosques in the Yemen, pl. 12.

[42] S. Flury, Ornamental Kufic inscriptions on pottery. *A Survey of Persian Art*, A.U. Pope, ed., IV, London, 1964-5, 1743-70, fig. 617.

Thus it seems that the inscription closest to this one is that on the *maqṣūra* of Sidi 'Uqbā in the Great Mosque of Qairawān which bears the name of Abū Tamīm al-Mu'izz ibn Bādīs.[43] Flury suggests in his conclusion that the *maqṣūra* was probably built by an Iraqi artist.[44] Flury's argument is based on the fact that inscriptions with certain similarities to this were found in Amida and that since the Zirids broke away from the Fatimids and declared their allegiance to the Abbasids of Iraq, with whom they exchanged gifts, an Iraqi artist might have gone to Qairawān and have been responsible for the carving of the *maqṣūra*.[45] Flury makes no mention of the already existing similar letters in Tunisia as seen on tombstones,[46] before al-Mu'izz transferred his allegiance to the Abbasids in 433/1041.

Other factors in this site, such as the shapes of tombstones, semi-circular arches, the projecting *miḥrāb*, a possibly pre-fabricated *miḥrāb*, as well as the similarity of the style of writing to the North African prototypes, indicate a migration of artists to the east, who brought their tradition with them and applied it on this site. This migration may be due to the Fatimids, vying with the Abbasids for the leadership of the Islamic world. In this struggle diplomacy and warfare were reinforced by a policy of trade and well organised propaganda supported by the university of al-Aẓhar and similar institutions all over the Islamic world. The Gujarati coast was one of the centres of such Fatimid influence.[47] As has been discussed in the survey report the whole concept is Islamic, although the craftsmen were Indian. However, the overall accuracy of the inscription and the style suggest an Arab, or Arabic-speaking, scribe at work.

THE TOMBSTONES

At this site we find two types of memorial. One (no. 11 in fig. 3, pl. 11) is a *stele*, square in plan, and the remainder are hollow prisms which may have served the purpose of sarcophagi. Rectangular *stelae* are rare and are so far found only in Turkey dated 614/1217-18,[48] which is later than the one on this site. In North Africa cylindrical headstones are very common, and represent a very similar form of free standing memorial.[49] So far as the prism is concerned, a simple form is found on the tomb of Subuktagīn and As'ad ibn 'Alī at Ghazna.[50] More complete is the analogy with the Hammadid tombs[51] and others in Tunisia,[52] Sicily,[53] and Spain.[54] All these occurrences manifestly represent North African practice. The only examples outside North African influence are found in Turkey.[55]

Tomb no. 1 (no. 1 in fig. 3, pl. 11a)

The inscriptions on this tomb are written in two styles: the uppermost band in plaited, and the lower ones in floriated Kufic. The plaited Kufic inscription, which is better preserved, is of good penmanship and contains Quranic verses (*Qur'ān* IX, 21 and 22). The lower bands have been eroded, and only certain letters with swan-neck endings and floral motifs can be seen. Although the floriated style has its parallel in the west, the plaited style seems to have originated in the east, and not travelled far to the west. In her study on plaited Kufic, Lisa Volov found that the earliest evidence for the plaited rectangular letter appears on a Samanid coin (908-932), the next on a coin minted in Ray (324/935-6), and in the course of the 10th and 11th centuries on coins of the Samanids, Buids, Ghaznavids and Seljuqs.[56] This practice which must

---

[43] According to Flury the *maqṣūra* belongs to the period between 406-53/1016-61 (see Flury, *Amida-Diarbekr*, 35), however, since the name Abū Tamīm appears on it, it must belong to the period when Abū Tamīm conducted the business of state alone although his father was still alive, between the years 449/1057 and 454/1062 (see *EI*, Tamīm b. al-Mu'izz) or after 454/1062 when he officially became the sovereign.

[44] Flury, *Amida-Diarbekr*, 35.

[45] *Ibid.*

[46] El-Habib, *Stèles funéraires*, fig. 22 no. 41b; fig. 32 no. 41; fig. 34 no. 41, fig. 39, no. 41a.

[47] B. Lewis, The Fatimids and the route to India, *Revue de la faculté des sciences économiques de l'Université d'Istanbul*, Istanbul, 1949-50, no. 1, 50-54.

[48] Beyhan Karamağarali, *Ahlat Mezartaslari*, Ankara, 1972, pl. 68, no. 146.

[49] El-Habib, *op. cit.*, pls. 2-15.

[50] Flury, *Ghazni*, pls. 6 and 19.

[51] L. Golvin, *Recherches Archéologiques à la Qal'a des Banū Ḥammād*, Paris, 1965, 159 fig. 57, and El-Habib, *op. cit.*, pl. 16.

[52] S.M. Zbiss, *Inscriptions de Gorjani*, Tunis, 1962, nos. 1-4; Zbiss, *Corpus*, pl. 13 no. 3; pl. 14. nos. 4 and 5; pl. 15 no. 6; pl. 16 no. 10; pl. 17, nos. 11 and 12; pl. 18 no. 13; pl. 20 no. 16; pl. 21 nos 17 and 18; pl. 22 no. 20; pl. 27 nos. 31 and 32.

[53] M. Amari, *Le epigrafi di Sicilia*, nos. 7; 10; 25 and 26.

[54] M.O. Jiminez, *Repertorio inscripciones Arabes de Almeria*, Madrid-Granada, 1964, pl. 18 no. 40; pl. 19 nos. 43-5; pl. 20 nos. 47-9; pl. 26 nos 77-8; pl. 34 nos. 80-1; pl. 36 no. 83; pl. 37 no. 84.

[55] Karamağarali, *Ahlat Mezartaslari*, 37, fig. 3; pl. 33 no. 72; pl. 52 no. 113; pl. 54 no. 118; pl. 56 no 123; pl. 57 no. 125; pl. 60 no. 131; pl. 61 nos 132-3; pl. 62 nos. 134-5.

[56] L. Volov, Plaited Kufic, 119.

have been the prototype for plaiting of the vertical strokes occurs under dynasties whose centre of power lay in the north-eastern and central provinces of Iran. In this particular region we also find the use of plaiting not only in the rectangular letters, but also in the vertical strokes, or merely as decoration placed between the letters, as seen on the inscriptions of the Arch of Bust,[57] the tomb of Bābā Ḥātam,[58] Imām Khurd,[59] the minaret of Ghazna[60] (all in Afghanistan), on the inscription of the Rādkān tower in Gurgān province,[61] and at the Pīr-i 'Alamdār in Dāmghān.[62] This feature is also seen in the inscriptions of an unglazed tile from Afrāsiyāb,[63] and slip painted pottery found in Nīshāpūr,[64] on a bronze bucket from Herat,[65] and on brass ewers from Khurasan.[66] However, towards the middle of the 6th/12th century a more developed form of plaiting appears in north-western Iran, where all vertical letters are intertwined in order to produce a continuous plaiting above the main baseline. These occur in the inscriptions of the Gulpāygān mosque (6th/12th century),[67] the Gunbad-i Surkh (542/1147-8),[68] the Gunbad-i Kabūd (563/1167-8),[69] and in the Si Gunbad (580/1184-5)[70] (all three in Marāgha in Azarbayjan), and on a pen case of brass from north-west Iran.[71] This move from the east to the west does not stop in Azarbayjan but is carried to Turkey where plaiting is seen in the Kara Tai Madrasa (649/1251-2),[72] and on the Ince Mināra (650-684/1252-85).[73] A similar movement is seen further in the east where it is found on the inscriptions of the screen facade of the Quwwat al-Islām mosque (596/1199),[74] and the Aṛhaī din kā Jhoṅpṛā mosque in Ajmer (started in 596/1200).[75] It is interesting to note that this style is not found in the west before the 8th/14th century where it appears in Spain,[76] and Morocco.[77] The only example of plaited letters in Egypt is on the inscriptions of the tomb of Imām Shāfi'ī (608/1211).[78] Thus it seems that this particular inscription, the only one of its kind, was probably executed by a craftsman familiar with the kind of art used in north-eastern Iran. It is not, however, surprising to find inscriptions of differing origins in a port which was the site of the shrine of a holy person, probably of a *shī'a* sect, and which attracted merchants and pilgrims.

Since the lower bands of the inscription have been eroded, neither the name of the deceased nor the date can be determined. However, by comparison with other inscriptions of similar style found elsewhere, this inscription can be dated to the late 6th/12th century.

Tomb no. 2 (no. 11 in fig. 3, pl. 11)

Unlike that of the previous tombstone, the inscription on this tomb is in a crudely written form of floriated Kufic with scroll decoration in the background. The inscription reads:[79]

---

[57] Daniel Schlumberger, *Lashkari Bazar, une résidence royale ghaznévide et ghoride, l'architecture*, Mémoires de la Délégation Archéologique Française en Afghanistan, XVIII, part IA, pl. 46b; M. Shokoohy, *Studies in the Early Mediaeval Architecture of Iran and Afghanistan*, Ph. D. Thesis for Heriot-Watt University, Edinburgh, 1978, pls. 144a and b.

[58] A.S. Melikian-Chirvani, Baba Hatim, un chef d'œuvre inconnu d'époque ghaznévide en Afghanistan, *The Memorial Volume of the Fifth International Congress of Iranian Art and Archaeology, 11th-18th April, 1968*, vol. 2, Teheran, 1972, 113.

[59] A.D.H. Bivar, Seljuqid *zīyārats* of Sar-i Pul (Afghanistan), *Bulletin of the School of Oriental and African Studies*, XXIX, 1966, pls. 2-9.

[60] Flury, *Ghazni*, 77.

[61] Flury, *Amida-Diarbekr*, pl. 14.

[62] Pope, *A Survey of Persian Art*, IV, 1723, fig. 588; and A.U. Pope, The painted inscription on the interior of the Pīr-i 'Alamdār of Damghan, *Bulletin of the American Institute for Persian Art and Archaeology*, IV, no. 3, June 1936, 141.

[63] A.U. Pope, *A Survey of Persian Art*, IV, 1731, fig. 595.

[64] Y. Ghulam, *Examples of Calligraphy in the Arts of Islamic Iran*, (s.a.), 8.

[65] *The Arts of Islam*, Catalogue of the Exhibition at the Hayward Gallery, 8th April-4th July 1976, The Arts Council of Great Britain, London, 1976, fig. 180.

[66] *Ibid.*, fig 188; and A.U. Pope, The Third International Congress and Exhibition for Iranian Art and Archaeology, *Bulletin of the American Institute for Persian Art and Archaeology*, V, no. 2, Dec. 1935, 63.

[67] A.U. Pope, *A Survey of Persian Art*, VIII, pl. 365c; and Y. Ghulam, *Introduction to the Art of Arabic Calligraphy in Iran*, The Asia Institute, Pahlavi University, Shiraz, (s.a.), 87.

[68] *Āthār-i Īrān*, I, Paris, 1936, 134.

[69] *Ibid.*, 136-7.

[70] *Ibid.*, 157.

[71] *The Arts of Islam*, fig. 193.

[72] S.H. Eldem, *Turk mimari eserleri*, Istanbul, (s.a.) pl. 38.

[73] *Ibid.*,pl. 39, the same practice is also found on the shrine of Kaykāwūs in Sivās, see pls. 40 and 41.

[74] Percy Brown, *Indian Architecture (Islamic Period)*, 5th ed. Bombay, 1968, 10t; T. Yamamoto et al., *Delhi*, I, Tokyo, 1967, pl. 6b.

[75] A. Cunningham, *ASIR*, 1862-8, II, pl. 74; M. Shokoohy, *Rajasthan*, I, Corpus Inscriptionum Iranicarum, Part IV, XLIX, London, 1986, pls. 3-7.

[76] E. Kühnel, *Islamische Schriftskunst*, Berlin-Leipzig (s.a.), 29, fig. 27.

[77] D. Hill and L. Golvin, *Islamic Architecture in North Africa*, London, 1976, figs. 313 and 543.

[78] The inscription of the tomb has not yet been published.

[79] Parts of this inscription are read from Dr. Desai's rubbing.

هذالقبر العبد الضعيف الراجى الى / رحمه الله لزاهدا(؟) ابو الفرج بن على السيرافى توفى بتاريخ يوم الثلاثه العشرين من شهر شعبان / فى شهور سنه تسعه (*sic*) ستين خمسمائه /

"This is the tomb of the weak servant, hoping for the mercy of God, for a self-denying (?), Abu'l-faraj, son of 'Alī al-Sīrāfī. He died on Tuesday, the 20th of the month of *sha'bān*, in the year 569 (26th March 1174)".

Tomb no. 3 (pl. 46)

The inscription on this tombstone is written in a crude floriated Kufic with the tails of the letters ending in swan-neck form. Scattered floral decoration is also used in the background. The inscription reads:

[بسـ]ـم الله الرحمن الرحيم / لا اله الا هو كل شى ها لك الا وجهه له الحكم / و اليه ترجعون كل نفس ذائقه الموت لا اله الا الله محمد رسول الله / هذا لقبر (*sic*) لعبد (*sic*) الضعيف .... الى رحمه الله تعالى سومر بن فرها .... / توفى [بـ]تاريخ شهر جمادى الاول فى شهور سنه ثلاث و سبعين و خمس مئه /

"*Qur'ān*, XXVIII, 88; III, 184. (Followed by) There is no God but God, Muḥammad is the messenger of God. This is the tomb of the weak servant ...[80] of the mercy of the exalted God, Sumra, son of Farhā... He died in the month of *jumādā I*, the year 573 (October-November 1177)".

Tomb no. 4 (pl. 47a)

This inscription is written in floriated Kufic of a much better quality than the previous two. The inscription reads:

بتاريخ يوم / الجمعه عشرين / من شهر شعبان سنه اربع / و العشرين [وستـ] مئه /

"On Friday, 20th of the month of *sha'bān*, the year [6]24 (5th August 1227)".

Tomb no. 5 (pl. 47b)

From what one can see of the inscription, the style is floriated Kufic, and as on Tomb no. 3, crudely written. The inscription reads:

"... He died in ... 62[?] (1224-31)".

.... توفى بتاريخ .... والعشرين و ستمائه

CONCLUSION

The monument at Bhadreśvar known locally as the Dargāh of La'l Shahbāz is referred to in this study as the Shrine of Ibrāhīm after Dr. Desai's reading of the inscriptions. These inscriptions do not in fact support the theory that the monument is a tomb, and it would simply appear to have been constructed by a certain Ibrāhīm, whom we cannot identify with any certainty. However, the size of the building, the presence of a *miḥrāb*, the use of the Throne Verse, and the existence of a graveyard around the building, all indicate that it had a religious, probably funerary, function. The stylistic resemblance of the inscription to those of North Africa, the shape of the tombstones, the projection of the back wall of the *miḥrāb*, which possibly had a *miḥrāb* of another material on the interior, and the round arch are all factors which relate the community for whom this building was constructed to North Africa. As this site was a port, there could well have been a trade connection with North Africa, an immigration at the time of the breaking up of a political centre into *shī'a* and *sunnī*, or a settlement as part of the Fatimid policy of trade and propaganda in Gujarat during the 11th century. The only non-North African inscription is that of Tomb no. 1, whose style is related to a north-eastern Iranian prototype. One might even be inclined to conclude that because this site had become a *shī'a* centre, migrations from the north had also occurred, and this might explain the presence of an Iranian influence. Local craftsmen were also employed, the result of their work being evident on the crudely written inscriptions on Tombs nos. 2, 3, and 5. These inscriptions appear to imitate stylistically those on the shrine.

[80] Dr. Desai read the word I have omitted here as *rājī* "hoping". Although this would be the right word in this context, the word actually written is not *rājī*, but a word like *'āṣir* "presser", or *'āṣī* "sinner", neither of which makes sense. One is therefore inclined to take this as being a mistake of the craftsman.

INDEX

LIST OF ILLUSTRATIONS

FIGURES

PLATES

Pl. 16b Solahkhambī Masjid, remains of the western colonnade and the western wall from the south-west.
Pl. 17a Solahkhambī Masjid, remains of the main *miḥrāb*.
Pl. 17b Solahkhambī Masjid, the portico in front of the entrance, showing the secondary *miḥrāb*.
Pl. 18a Solahkhambī Masjid, the *miḥrāb* in the portico.
Pl. 18b Solahkhambī Masjid, column at the south-western corner of the courtyard.
Pl. 19a Solahkhambī Masjid, columns with different types of ante-capitals at the north-western corner of the courtyard. A corbelled stone set in the wall to support the lintel can be seen on the right.
Pl. 19b Solahkhambī Masjid, detail of columns in the western colonnade.
Pl. 20a Solahkhambī Masjid, remains of a decorated stone of the jamb of the entrance.
Pl. 20b Solahkhambī Masjid, eave stones used at a later date to wall up the portico.
Pl. 21a Solahkhambī Masjid, later structure forming a new entrance at the northern side of the portico, cutting into one of the columns.
Pl. 21b Solahkhambī Masjid, the ancient column reused in later alterations to the mosque.
Pl. 21c Solahkhambī Masjid, remains of a Jain altar installed in the south side of the portico at a later date.
Pl. 22a Chhoṭī Masjid, southern view.
Pl. 22b Chhoṭī Masjid, northern view.
Pl. 23a Chhoṭī Masjid, eastern view showing the main entrance, and behind it the secondary chamber built inside the courtyard.
Pl. 23b Chhoṭī Masjid, western view.
Pl. 24a Chhoṭī Masjid, view from the courtyard towards the south-west corner of the colonnade. The south entrance of the colonnade can also be seen walled up with blocks of stone.
Pl. 24b Chhoṭī Masjid, view from the courtyard towards the north-west corner of the colonnade.
Pl. 25a Chhoṭī Masjid, view of the upper part of the front of the colonnade, showing the structural units of the roof.
Pl. 25b Chhoṭī Masjid, interior view of the colonnade looking towards the south.
Pl. 26a Chhoṭī Masjid, southern wall of the colonnade and its arched entrance, now blocked.
Pl. 26b Chhoṭī Masjid, the *miḥrāb* of the western wall of the colonnade.
Pl. 27a Chhoṭī Masjid, northern entrance from the colonnade to the chamber.
Pl. 27b Chhoṭī Masjid, southern entrance from the colonnade to the chamber.
Pl. 28a Chhoṭī Masjid, details of the upper part of a column in the colonnade.
Pl. 28b Chhoṭī Masjid, interior view of the chamber looking towards the south-west.
Pl. 29a Chhoṭī Masjid, northern wall of the chamber, interior view.
Pl. 29b Chhoṭī Masjid, southern view of the chamber and its engaged column, interior view.
Pl. 30a Chhoṭī Masjid, two of the columns in the chamber.
Pl. 30b Chhoṭī Masjid, base of a column in the chamber.
Pl. 31a Chhoṭī Masjid, upper parts of a column and two of the decorated lintels in the chamber.
Pl. 31b Chhoṭī Masjid, lotus decoration on the lower side of a lintel in the chamber.
Pl. 32a Chhoṭī Masjid, the *miḥrāb* in the chamber.
Pl. 32b Chhoṭī Masjid, exterior view of the *miḥrāb* of the chamber, showing part of the decoration around the roof and under the drip stones, and two of the water spouts.
Pl. 33a Chhoṭī Masjid, secondary chamber built in the courtyard at a later date. Exterior view of the northern wall showing the entrance.
Pl. 33b Chhoṭī Masjid, interior view of the secondary chamber showing the unfinished arches.
Pl. 34a The Chatri, general view from the east.
Pl. 34b The Chatri, general view from the west.
Pl. 35 The Chatri, columns at the north-west corner.
Pl. 36a The Chatri, interior view of the dome.
Pl. 36b The Chatri, interior view of the dome.
Pl. 37a The Chatri, detail of decoration on one of the stub lintels.
Pl. 37b The Chatri, base of a column.
Pl. 38a Dūdhā Wāv, general view from the west, showing all three remaining bridges.
Pl. 38b Dūdhā Wāv, view of the two bridges.
Pl. 39a Dūdhā Wāv, view from the east towards the west.
Pl. 39b Dūdhā Wāv, view from the north towards the south.
Pl. 40a Dūdhā Wāv, view from the west.
Pl. 40b Dūdhā Wāv, detail of the joints of the roof lintels at the eastern bridge.
Pl. 41a Dūdhā Wāv, detail of the corbels at the south-eastern corner.
Pl. 41b Dūdhā Wāv, view of the east wall showing the opening to the well shaft in the lower part of the wall, and the six corbels in the upper part.
Pl. 42a Dūdhā Wāv, columns at the eastern bridge.
Pl. 42b Dūdhā Wāv, remains of the well to the east side of the reservoir.
Pl. 43 Dated inscription of the Shrine of Ibrāhīm, a to c: beginning of the inscription on the western wall of the portico.
Pl. 44 Dated inscription of the Shrine of Ibrāhīm, a: continuation of the inscription on the southern wall of the portico; b and c: on the northern part of the lintels at the eastern side of the portico.
Pl. 45 Dated inscription of the Shrine of Ibrāhīm, a and b: continuation of the inscription on the southern part of the lintels at the eastern side of the portico; c: end of the inscription on the northern wall of the portico.
Pl. 46 a and b Tomstone lying to the west of the Solahkhambī Masjid and bearing the date *jamādā al-awwal* 573/October-November 1177.
Pl. 47a Tombstone dated 20th *sha'bān* [6]24/5th August 1227, now lying near the Solahkhambī Masjid.
Pl. 47b Tombstone to the north of the Solahkhambī Masjid bearing the date 62[?]/1224-31.
Pl. 48a Junagadh, the Mosque of Al-Īrajī, view from the north-east.
Pl. 48b The Mosque of al-Īrajī, view from the north.
Pl. 49a The Mosque of al-Īrajī, view from the north showing the ancient cave under the mosque.
Pl. 49b The Mosque of al-Īrajī, the northern end of the portico. The inscription is carved on the lintel over the central entrance.
Pl. 50a The Mosque of al-Īrajī, view from the south-west showing the solid decorative dome above the *miḥrāb* and the entrance, now blocked, to the south chamber.
Pl. 50b The Mosque of al-Īrajī, southern wall of the southern chamber and the portico, from the south-east.

Pl. 51a The Mosque of al-Īrajī, semi-circular projection of the *miḥrāb* behind the *qibla* wall.
Pl. 51b The Mosque of al-Īrajī, exterior view of the northern entrance.
Pl. 52a The Mosque of al-Īrajī, view of the northern entrance from the courtyard.
Pl. 52b The Mosque of al-Īrajī, view towards the northern end of the portico.
Pl. 53a The Mosque of al-Īrajī, view towards the southern end of the portico.
Pl. 53b The Mosque of al-Īrajī, the *qibla* wall and the *miḥrāb*.
Pl. 54a The Mosque of al-Īrajī, interior view of the southern wall of the sanctuary.
Pl. 54b The Mosque of al-Īrajī, the southern chamber, looking towards the partition wall, with one of the windows to the sanctuary on the right.
Pl. 55a The Mosque of al-Īrajī, the sanctuary, interior view showing the central entrance.
Pl. 55b The Mosque of al-Īrajī, eastern window of the southern wall of the sanctuary, seen from the south chamber.
Pl. 56a-c The Mosque of al-Īrajī, inscription, line 1.
Pl. 57a The Mosque of al-Īrajī, inscription, end of line 1.
Pl. 57b The Mosque of al-Īrajī, inscription, line 2, right side.
Pl. 57c The Mosque of al-Īrajī, inscription, line 2, left side.
Pl. 58a and b Junagadh, the step-well carved into the rock to the east of the Mosque of al-Īrajī.

Site of ancient Bhadreśvar, view from the south.

PLATE 2

a) Bhadreśvar, the Shrine of Ibrāhīm, southern view of the enclosure.

b) The Shrine of Ibrāhīm, eastern façade.

a) The Shrine of Ibrāhīm, northern corner of the portico.

b) The Shrine of Ibrāhīm, the entrance under the portico.

PLATE 4

a) The Shrine of Ibrāhīm, view from the south-east.

b) The Shrine of Ibrāhīm, upper parts of a column and a pilaster in the portico.

a) The Shrine of Ibrāhīm, western window at the northern side.

b) The Shrine of Ibrāhīm, western window at the southern side.

PLATE 6

a) The Shrine of Ibrāhīm, decoration on the ante-capital of a column in the portico.

b) The Shrine of Ibrāhīm, decoration on one of the lintels of the portico.

a) The Shrine of Ibrāhīm, the ceiling of the portico.

b) The Shrine of Ibrāhīm, western view.

a) The Shrine of Ibrāhīm, interior view.

b) The Shrine of Ibrāhīm, view of the *qibla* wall and the *miḥrāb*.

a) The Shrine of Ibrāhīm, interior view looking towards the north-eastern corner.

b) The Shrine of Ibrāhīm, detail of the pilaster capitals, the ante-capitals, and the lintels inside the chamber.

Plate 10

a) The Shrine of Ibrāhīm, interior view of the dome.

b) The Shrine of Ibrāhīm, interior view of the dome.

a) The Shrine of Ibrāhīm, tombs to the west of the shrine (nos. 1, 2, and 11 in fig. 3).

b) The Shrine of Ibrāhīm, north-western view, showing the tombs to the north and to the west of the shrine.

PLATE 12

Bhadreśvar, Solahkhambī Masjid, view from the south.

a) Solahkhambī Masjid, view from the north-west.

b) Solahkhambī Masjid, remains of the portico and the eastern colonnade.

a) Solahkhambī Masjid, southern view.

b) Solahkhambī Masjid, northern view. The topping stone of a tomb can be seen above the present ground level in the foreground.

a) Solahkhambī Masjid, standing wall of the northern side. Drip stones can be seen scattered on the ground.

b) Solahkhambī Masjid, ornamental antefixae around the upper edge of the northern wall.

a) Solahkhambī Masjid, remains of the western colonnade and the western wall from the south.

b) Solahkhambī Masjid, remains of the western colonnade and the western wall from the south-west.

a) Solahkhambī Masjid, remains of the main *miḥrāb*.

b) Solahkhambī Masjid, the portico in front of the entrance, showing the secondary *miḥrāb*.

PLATE 18

a) Solahkhambi Masjid, the *miḥrāb* in the portico.

b) Solahkhambī Masjid, column at the south-western corner of the courtyard.

a) Solahkhambī Masjid, columns with different types of ante-capitals at the north-western corner of the courtyard. A corbelled stone set in the wall to support the lintel can be seen on the right.

b) Solahkhambī Masjid, detail of columns in the western colonnade.

PLATE 20

a) Solahkhambī Masjid, remains of a decorated stone of the jamb of the entrance.

b) Solahkhambī Masjid, eave stones used at a later date to wall up the portico.

a) Solahkhambī Masjid, later structure forming a new entrance at the northern side of the portico, cutting into one of the columns.

b) Solahkhambī Masjid, the ancient column reused in later alterations to the mosque.

c) Solahkhambī Masjid, remains of a Jain altar installed in the south side of the portico at a later date.

PLATE 22

a) Chhoṭī Masjid, southern view.

b) Chhoṭī Masjid, northern view.

a) Chhoṭī Masjid, eastern view showing the main entrance, and behind it the secondary chamber built inside the courtyard.

b) Chhoṭī Masjid, western view.

PLATE 24

a) Chhoṭī Masjid, view from the courtyard towards the south-west corner of the colonnade. The south entrance of the colonnade can also be seen walled up with blocks of stone.

b) Chhoṭī Masjid, view from the courtyard towards the north-west corner of the colonnade.

a) Chhoṭī Masjid, view of the upper part of the front of the colonnade, showing the structural units of the roof.

b) Chhoṭī Masjid, interior view of the colonnade looking towards the south.

a) Chhoṭī Masjid, southern wall of the colonnade and its arched entrance, now blocked.

b) Chhoṭī Masjid, the *miḥrāb* of the western wall of the colonnade.

a) Chhoṭī Masjid, northern entrance from the colonnade to the chamber.

b) Chhoṭī Masjid, southern entrance from the colonnade to the chamber.

a) Chhoṭī Masjid, details of the upper part of a column in the colonnade.

b) Chhoṭī Masjid, interior view of the chamber looking towards the south-west.

a) Chhoṭī Masjid, northern wall of the chamber, interior view.

b) Chhoṭī Masjid, southern view of the chamber and its engaged column, interior view.

a) Chhoṭī Masjid, two of the columns in the chamber.

b) Chhoṭī Masjid, base of a column in the chamber.

a) Chhoṭī Masjid, upper parts of a column and two of the decorated lintels in the chamber.

b) Chhoṭī Masjid, lotus decoration on the lower side of a lintel in the chamber.

a) Chhoṭī Masjid, the *miḥrāb* in the chamber.

b) Chhoṭī Masjid, exterior view of the *miḥrāb* of the chamber, showing part of the decoration around the roof and under the drip stones, and two of the water spouts.

a) Chhoṭī Masjid, secondary chamber built in the courtyard at a later date. Exterior view of the northern wall showing the entrance.

b) Chhoṭī Masjid, interior view of the secondary chamber showing the unfinished arches.

PLATE 34

a) The Chatri, general view from the east.

b) The Chatri, general view from the west.

The Chatri, columns at the north-west corner.

a) The Chatri, interior view of the dome.

b) The Chatri, interior view of the dome.

a) The Chatri, detail of decoration on one of the stub lintels.

b) The Chatri, base of a column.

a) Dūdhā Wāv, general view from the west, showing all three remaining bridges.

b) Dūdhā Wāv, view of two of the bridges.

a) Dūdhā Wāv, view from the east towards the west.

b) Dūdhā Wāv, view from the north towards the south.

a) Dūdhā Wāv, view from the west.

b) Dūdhā Wāv, detail of the joints of the roof lintels at the eastern bridge.

a) Dūdhā Wāv, detail of the corbels at the south-eastern corner.

b) Dūdhā Wāv, view of the east wall showing the opening to the well shaft in the lower part of the wall, and the six corbels in the upper part.

a) Dūdhā Wāv, columns at the eastern bridge.

b) Dūdhā Wāv, remains of the well to the east side of the reservoir.

a

b

c

Dated inscription of the Shrine of Ibrāhīm: (a) to (c) beginning of the inscription on the western wall of the portico.

a

b

c

Dated inscription of the Shrine of Ibrāhīm, (a) continuation of the inscription on the northern wall of the portico; (b) and (c) on the southern part of the lintels at the eastern side of the portico.

a

b

c

Dated inscription of the Shrine of Ibrāhīm, (a) and (b) continuation of the inscription on the southern part of the lintels at the eastern side of the portico; (c) end of the inscription on the northern wall of the portico.

a

b

a) and b) Tombstone lying to the west of the Solahkhambī Masjid and bearing the date *jamādā al-awwal* 573/October-November 1177.

a) Tombstone dated 20th *sha'bān* [6]24/5th August 1227, now lying near the Solahkhambī Masjid.

b) Tombstone to the north of the Solahkhambī Masjid bearing the date 62[?]1224-31.

PLATE 48

a) Junagadh, the Mosque of al-Īrajī, view from the north-east.

b) The Mosque of al-Īrajī, view from the north.

a) The Mosque of al-Īrajī, view from the north showing the ancient cave under the mosque.

b) The Mosque of al-Īrajī, the northern end of the portico. The inscription is carved on the lintel over the central entrance.

a) The Mosque of al-Īrajī, view from the south-west showing the solid decorative dome above the *miḥrāb* and the entrance, now blocked, to the south chamber.

b) The Mosque of al-Īrajī, southern wall of the south chamber and the portico, from the south-east.

a) The Mosque of al-Īrajī, semi-circular projection of the *miḥrāb* behind the *qibla* wall.

b) The Mosque of al-Īrajī, exterior view of the northern entrance.

a) The Mosque of al-Īrajī, view of the northern entrance from the courtyard.

b) The Mosque of al-Īrajī, view towards the northern end of the portico.

a) The Mosque of al-Īrajī, view towards the southern end of the portico.

b) The Mosque of al-Īrajī, the *qibla* wall and the *miḥrāb*.

PLATE 54

a) The Mosque of al-Īrajī, interior view of the southern wall of the sanctuary.

b) The Mosque of al-Īrajī, the southern chamber, looking towards the partition wall, with one of the windows to the sanctuary on the right.

a) The Mosque of al-Īrajī, the sanctuary, interior view showing the central entrance.

b) The Mosque of al-Īrajī, eastern window of the southern wall of the sanctuary, seen from the south chamber.

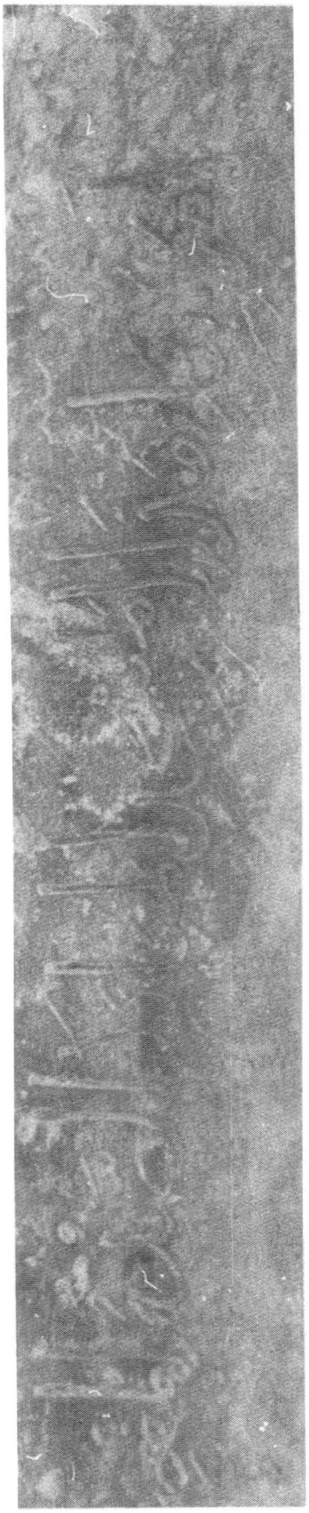

a

b

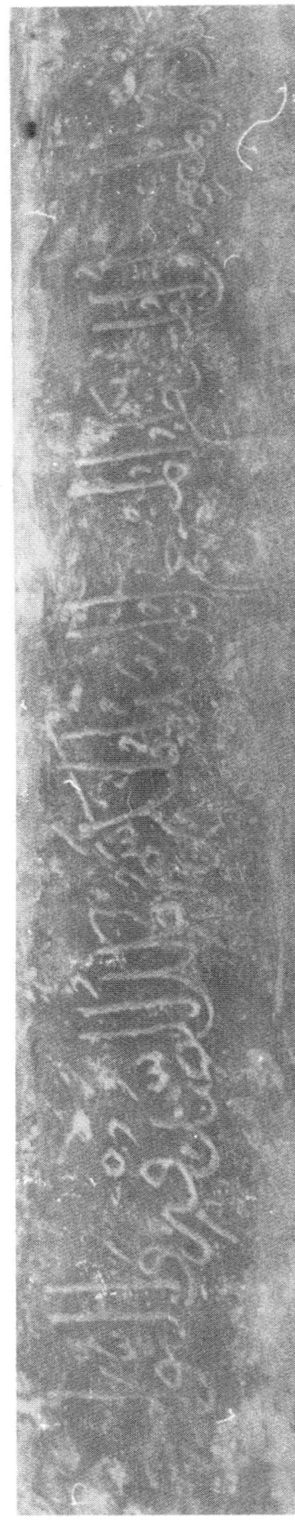

c

a), b), c) The Mosque of al-Īrajī, inscription line 1.

a) The Mosque of al-Īrajī, inscription, end of line 1.

b) The Mosque of al-Īrajī, inscription line 2, right side.

c) The Mosque of al-Īrajī, inscription line 2, left side.

PLATE 58

a) and b) Junagadh, the step-well carved into the rock to the east of the Mosque of al-Īrajī.